Sober

AND

Miserable

by Dale Simpson

Copyright © 2013 by Dale Simpson

All rights reserved.

ISBN: 0982773757
ISBN-13: 9780982773758

Published by Perfected Pen Publishing.
www.PerfectedPen.com
www.SabrinaKCarpenter.com

PREFACE

In August of 1970, several ugly facts intruded their way into my life. My drinking was out of control. My life had become unmanageable…by me, anyway. But, the state of Ohio was thinking about taking over that responsibility for me.

I was at a crossroads. Either I could stop drinking all together or face a life where the certainties all seemed to be unpleasant. Amazingly enough, I decided to stop drinking with the help of AA, counselors, family and friends. My initial recovery was nearly stellar. I was 23 and my physical health returned very quickly. My confidence and motivation came back with a vengeance. I was on the road to a life free of alcohol that, to this day, has continued for more than 40 years.

I had become imbued with the thought that abstinence from alcohol was the secret to happiness. I was told over and over that if I didn't drink today, everything would be okay. It was becoming apparent that the program was full of wisdom and very effective at getting people to stop drinking for good. There was excellent support available for newcomers to recovery, including thousands of meetings and an extensive supply of written material. The overwhelming majority of it is aimed at the new person. This seemed to be an assumption that once we've overcome our tendencies to drink, everything will proceed smoothly. I received extensive training and support to say that everything is okay whenever I was asked. The longer one is sober, the more he is expected to project success with his program of recovery. Talking a good game is a highly valued skill. But, many times, they are empty words.

Here's the rub. The longer I've been sober, the more I've been made aware of people with lengthy periods of sobriety that are very unhappy just below their very sober surface. My initial thoughts about writing about this particular topic revolved around the possibility of sharing my observations of others in their struggles with recovery and happiness. I've known many people who have suffered with emotional and mental problems deep into their years of sobriety. I thought it might be a service to the community at large to share how they handled, or didn't handle, their troubles within the context of recovery. They are examples of how a person long into sobriety can address their problems and find happiness. I was to be the observer and reporter.

It really didn't take too long for me to see that reporting the troubles of others had severe limitations. First, I had to deal with the issues of my own biases and the judgments I would be making on the individuals I was discussing. While I thought these people were displaying misery in their lives, I could have easily been wrong. Even in the cases where people confided in me about their difficulties, I had to deal with the implied confidentiality they expected when they shared these things. Even though it appeared to me that the majority of people in long-term sobriety were suffering and had deep issues that were unaddressed, it became apparent that I couldn't use them for the basis of my discussions. Many of these people would be too easy to identify.

In the end, the solution was fairly simple. I had over 40 years of experience with a recovering person whom I knew intimately. I was also completely aware of his mood, his state of mind and his level of happiness. That person, of course, would be me. I realized I was actually a pretty good candidate for this study. I had gotten to recovery young. I had stayed abstinent for many years without interruption. I was well educated in the literature and practice of 12 step programs. I had stayed active in

Preface

12 step programs for over 40 years. I had also achieved moderate measure of material success. In the conventional sense, I "should" be happy.

Something that has occasionally bothered me in life, was that in most ways, I was just average. A normal kind of guy. And AA regularly reinforced the notion that we are not unique. Keeping this in mind, I submit to you the following pages that describe the development of my life from an utterly self-centered, young, alcoholic and drug addict to a much older, peaceful and loving person in recovery. My journey was not linear. There were many cavernous valleys. I spent a lot of time "faking it". I spent years in mild to moderate shame because I was sober but not happy. I use my own experience of suffering to differentiate what was and wasn't valuable about my life.

All of the events described are real. They happened. Some have been altered slightly to protect people who are still living. The events were selected because they have moved me away from my self-centered obsessions and character defects toward becoming a different and better person.

Is my deepest hope that my writing will help someone avoid the years of suffering that I endured. My life is now peaceful and I am able to love and be loved. I continue to practice my recovery program and a spiritual life on a daily basis. May everyone's life be improved by these words. May we all find peace in the living of our lives.

Dale Simpson

Chapter 1

Alcohol Isn't the Whole Problem

You might think that someone who was able to stop drinking alcohol and stay sober for more than 20 years, would have figured out how to be happy. In most cases, you would be wrong. The majority of people I have observed over the last 40 years have managed to escape the terrors of drinking but in spite of that, many of them have remained profoundly unhappy and dissatisfied with their lives. I believe this outcome is undesirable and avoidable. I have personally been granted full relief from this misery and have enjoyed spiritual and emotional freedom for over forty years. If my experience and observations can help any suffering individual achieve a sense of spiritual peace and freedom, I will be hugely grateful.

    The early years in recovery can be a joy and a nightmare. I stand in awe of all the individuals who have confronted an alcoholic life and have taken on the excruciatingly difficult task of recovery from this fatal disease. It takes many of us years, and repeated attempts at recovery before we are able to resist that temptation of the first drink. Then, the recovering alcoholic is faced with the task of reordering their entire lives. The people I am talking about have, in spite of all the obstacles, managed to find a way to move on with their lives without drink. They have learned a new way of living that allows them to have jobs, careers, relationships and even troubles.

Sober And Miserable

By the time I was 23, I had done a lifetime of drinking and troublemaking…or at least that's what the judge told me it looked like. The handwritten charge on the summons said "simple drunk". I had been arrested while on foot, and not in my car, because I was too drunk to find it. The next day, I had to call the police to find out where I had been arrested. That gave me a starting point to begin the search for my car. The sergeant I talked to said I should think about the impact my actions would have if it turned out that I had parked on someone's lawn and it had been towed.

Back to the courtroom…I plead guilty and the judge fined me $10. As I paid the check, the judge motioned me over to the bench. Just when I was feeling so good about the fine, my heart dropped to the floor. He leaned over and whispered to me, "You're too young to be such a mess. You should get your butt to AA. It's at 405 Oak Street."

I just stood there, I didn't know what to say or do. I just walked away. Shocked by his honesty. This was on a Thursday morning. I went to my first meeting that Friday night. It was August of 1970 and I have not had a drink since. Ultimately that $10 fine and the nosy judge, may well have saved my life.

The first three or four years in recovery can be quite a lot of fun. I finally found a group of people with whom I felt comfortable. I felt great relief and a sense of fellowship almost immediately. I was finally understood by people that I liked. There was a strong emotional connection that created an attraction for me to everyone around me that was trying to stay sober. The group of men that I hung out with were caring and helpful, without being pushy. If they pushed me, it was by teasing. They educated me in the fundamentals of recovery by showing me how they lived their lives without alcohol. The area that I was most afraid of was how I would have fun now that I didn't drink. They showed me firsthand by sharing their lives, their families and their entertainment. For the first time in my life, I was beginning to feel good about me and amazed

Chapter 1 – Alcohol Isn't The Whole Problem

that my compulsion to drink was leaving me. The wreckage of my life was beginning to fall away. Not creating new wreckage goes a long way towards making life manageable. People were even starting to trust me. My family and friends had begun to open their arms to me once again. During this period I enjoyed the simple peace that came from a life with a little discipline and less drama. I felt like whatever had been chasing me, had disappeared.

Yes, I mentioned that I had fun in early recovery. I did things I hadn't done for years. Our group in Cincinnati would meet with other young people from Columbus and Indianapolis on weekends and have meetings, dances and parties. I was more social than I had been in years. Maybe forever. I guess not throwing up on people or punching them somehow made me more attractive to them. I also started volunteering to make coffee, chair meetings and generally help out when I was asked. My recovery consisted of meetings, work, parties and trying to figure out what to do with my life. I dated pretty much any woman who would go out with me. This became an almost obsessive feature of my life. I didn't like being alone. When it came right down to it, I wasn't real comfortable being on a date, either.

My time was spent creating my future. I went to graduate school, got my master's degree and landed a very good internship. I was driven by the lure of the future and all the riches it would hold for me. I was firmly committed to being materially successful. That was the most fundamental of beliefs I held. I had other beliefs, such as a very strong sense of entitlement. I don't really know where they came from since I was raised in a fairly humble and happy family. Now it seemed my only focus, the only benchmark I had, was material success. And I was feeling like the good things that were happening were a result of my not drinking and my brilliant planning skills. For the first time in my life, I felt I was a winner. My friends and the people I was close to in my recovery fellowship reinforced these notions by constantly telling me how well I was doing and pointing out just how unusual it was for a person as young as I.

Sober And Miserable

As refreshing and wholesome as this early recovery seemed at times, pretty much everything of substance contained only the appearance of recovery. As far my character went, I was still the sneaky, clever, self-centered and manipulative child I had always been. It was obvious to me that the path of least resistance was to not drink, and to be seen with the right people in the fellowship. I had read all the literature and could quote it like an old hand. Appearing compliant was my strongest suit in the game of recovery. It wasn't that I was interested in deceiving anyone but I had no way to let anyone in. My insides were as unknown to me as the dark side of the Moon. An inch below the surface, I was resistant to any real change. I still had all the desires, delusions and character defects I had when I was drinking. After my first five years in recovery, I had gotten a pretty blonde wife, a master's degree, and a sports car in my first job as a hospital CEO. I was movin' and groovin'.

It wasn't that my friends in recovery didn't try to introduce me to a more substantial life. They tried every time I saw them. They earnestly tried to interest me in a God or spiritually-based life. I usually smiled and rolled my eyes. They were sober and old and needed the God stuff. Not me. I told myself I was sober and behaving pretty well compared to my past performances. The truth was that I wasn't drinking, but I wasn't behaving very well either. Every little slippery thing I did was rationalized in my mind. My guiding principle was, "It's a short life and you're dead a long time, so get it while you can!" This was kept very much to myself, of course. My belief was that no one was really honest anyway. My deepest feelings are that I would be left behind in this life if I played it straight.

For ten years, I cultivated an image of myself that was mainly for public consumption. I was sober, active in recovery, read the correct literature and was willing to share the message of recovery almost anywhere. I was constantly being congratulated for having such a good life. I was such a good boy. My outside appearance was my reality…or at least I tried to believe that ten years in, I had it all going on. I was asked to speak all around the country. Of course I accepted. By now, I had a

Chapter 1 – Alcohol Isn't The Whole Problem

beautiful family, great job, great house on seven acres, cars, a boat and a summer place on the lake in Vermont. I had my life the way I wanted it. I was in control.

When I look back at this time, while I was sober and proud of it, my behavior was deteriorating on almost a daily basis. The AA fellowship gives an individual many ways to re-form their lives. Most of them center around the discovery of spirituality within one's self and connecting that with a higher power. This concept was totally alien to me. My experience with religion to this point in my life had been neither good nor bad. There had simply been no inner connection for me. I went to church to please my parents. And although my father was, I believe, a spiritual man, it was not something we ever discussed. Add to that my perception of the religious fringe and their bizarre behavior, I could see little or no way that religion could serve any purpose in my life.

So, I took the easy way and showed up at mass on holidays and special occasions. Purely, for appearances. Without inner resources, I found it very difficult to live a principled life. As the calendar rolled forward, I had to work hard not to lose ground every day to fear and despair. I had found material success and it wasn't working. I needed something else but I didn't want to tell anybody how unhappy I was. I liked the image I had cultivated. That was nearly my undoing.

It's not even that during these early years I wasn't getting good advice. In fact, I was told on a regular basis that although I had some gifts and talents, there was no height they could take me that my character defects couldn't bring me down. I nodded, smiled and ignored the advice. I seriously couldn't believe that the advice applied to me. It seemed like another one of those academic discussions. It would be something good to know for future reference. And it was.

Unfortunately, as I got more deeply into my own drama and alcohol-free jackpots I was unable to remember all the good advice I have been given…and ignored. The only benchmarks I retained related to my material successes. From that perspective, I seemed to be doing quite well. It would take me almost 20 years in recovery to understand that my measuring stick was twisted and in reality served no good purpose.

In my 19th year, my self-centered, self-serving, careless ways all pretty much converged and took down my very superficial life. The principal illusion I had lived with was that everyone liked me and nobody knew about my transgressions. And of course, almost everyone knew who I was and was not very thrilled with that reality. In short order, I was divorced, unemployed, without a home and all alone. I would have almost a year of unemployment to contemplate my self-pity. I wanted someone to blame and avoided the knowledge that I was the only one culpable. This would be a very frightening year. In it, I would go from looking for somebody to blame, to the beginnings of understanding my own culpability. I finally started to look inside myself. What I saw was nearly overwhelming. Emotionally, this was a far worse bottom than the one that had brought me into recovery 19 years earlier. I could no longer hide from the facts of who I was. My pain was deep inside of me and I was miserable. The last thing I wanted to do was to deal with my hidden shortcomings in public with my friends and support group. When the pain got bad enough, I sought out my friends and asked for help.

The most uniform response I received was for me to surrender to God. Although I had no clue as to how to do that I decided I would try. I went to church, religious retreats, 12-step retreats, Dharma houses, gurus, priests, shamans and fortune tellers. I liked the fortune-tellers best. I think it is possible the fortune-tellers might have been trying to tell me what I wanted to hear. Oddly enough, all of my other attempts to find an entry point or common ground to meet God, left me cold and empty.

It didn't take all that long before I was thinking that it must be me that can't connect with anything. A little self-pity always helps. I wanted

Chapter 1 – Alcohol Isn't The Whole Problem

to believe in something but had no idea how to do that. The people around me in recovery constantly told me how much God was doing for them. He even paid their bills. Sent them checks. Provided them with romance, as well. Now I was really jealous. I was told to pray and to ask for whatever I needed. I tried but I couldn't even get a bicycle. I even tried prayers from my childhood. Tried and true, Catholic prayers. They didn't work either. It appeared that this God didn't want to hear from me. In many ways, I could understand that. I was by no means a model person.

The whole idea of God being a celestial vending machine really didn't sit very well with me. It just didn't feel right. I felt silly asking God for things I was perfectly able to get on my own. I was in serious trouble though, unable to find a God that I could connect with. I wanted something bigger than me to help me do whatever it was I was put on this earth to do. I had a pretty good idea that wasn't what I'd been doing so far. I had lived my 20 years in recovery in a completely selfish manner. I knew very little about giving and too much about taking. I knew that some kind of spiritual life might help but I felt like I was sowing those seeds on rock. I was feeling very helpless. This turned out to be a good thing.

One night when my youngest son was about seven, he and I lay in the grass in the backyard and we talked about the stars that were brilliantly visible on that dark night. It was bitter cold in northeastern Pennsylvania. We were having a very mellow conversation about what we could see. I asked him if he thought there was anything out there. He replied that there had to be…something that beautiful couldn't possibly be an accident.

"Dad?" he said. "I want to ask whoever made all of this, why he put it all so far away."

"Eric," I said, "I don't understand what you're getting at."

Sober And Miserable

"I heard on television that the closest galaxy to us was 34 light years away. People will never be able to get there. And everything else is further away!"

"What if we figure out how to go as fast as the speed of light?"

"They said that's not going to happen. Not even close."

"So, I guess we just get to appreciate them from a distance."

"That sucks! I really wanted to go there."

I feel like I have to mention this. A few years before this night of stargazing, Eric had been bitten on his hand by horse. His sister had been taking a riding lesson and his father had spaced out while he was supposed to be watching him. Eric good-naturedly tried to feed one of the horses an apple. We were soon on the way to the emergency room. His hand was cut up but one finger was particularly lacerated. Everyone in the ER knew Eric and made a big fuss over him. His mother worked in the lab three days a week. The regular ER doc wasn't there that night and his shift was being covered by a hand surgeon. When I met the doctor, he looked at Eric who was quite frightened at this point and said, "We've got to make sure this hand and finger work properly. Eric could be the first astronaut to leave the solar system." That moment came back to me years later after I had retrieved my higher power.

He had had no exposure to religion or arguments pro or con regarding God. He seemed to intuitively know that this was the work of some kind of Higher Power. The idea was simple and he was quite certain in his belief. And it warmed me deeply that he had this feeling inside. I was happy for him and wished I had even a little bit of his innocence. Maybe I just wasn't open to the possibility that I didn't know everything. Anything?

Chapter 1 – Alcohol Isn't The Whole Problem

There is a big price that has to be paid for the luxury of knowing everything. That debt is collected in the instant when you realize that you know almost nothing. And yet, that knowledge of how little we know can become the bedrock of the foundation for new life.

My nineteenth year in recovery brought me to my knees. Even though I couldn't pray while I was there, I finally began to accept the truths about me. As unattractive as those truths were, I finally had a place to begin living honestly. I knew that I didn't know much of anything and that was alright. There was comfort in the idea that I was starting fresh. Most of the serious work I had to do with spirituality wouldn't come until after I had confronted the demons that lived in the tangled belief system that guided my behavior throughout my life. Until that happened, I experienced a lot of frustration as I tried to grow spiritually. Much of that was a result of my unrealistic expectations. In most regards, I was still trying to control my life. When I started this process of attempting to grow spiritually after twenty years of faking it, I had little in the way of consciousness of my own feelings or those of others. I had a ton to learn.

This learning process had exposed me to many different ways to recover from my damaged beliefs and character defects. These lessons and experiences are what I want to share with everybody. I am absolutely certain that no one needs to take 20 years of misery or even serious discomfort before spiritual life opens up and allows us to experience all of what is good about life. The most difficult changes I had to make were letting go of old ideas and crippling beliefs. I had to become disciplined and conscious of my actions. This new way of life is far richer and fuller, completely without fear and finally open for joy. As simple as it was, for the most part, it was not intuitive. I needed a great deal of help and practice to stay on track with changes that were completely foreign to me.

Chapter 2

Finding My Inner Alcoholic

It was early in January and I was frosty coming home from catechism. This was after sister Norbert drained the last few drops of interest I ever had in Catholicism. It was also far too boring for my 11-year-old mind. We were told we had to come in after school because we were not fortunate enough to go to a Catholic school. Sister Norbert always smiled. I believe she'd still be smiling as she choked the very life out of you. Intuitively, I didn't trust her. One minute we were being told that we were a creation of a perfect God and then the next moment we could not be trusted to be left alone with our own bodies. Religion has never passed my own personal smell test. Today we had been treated to a film strip on what we could do if our parents weren't being good enough Catholics. After the film strip, she got very stern and asked if we would like to help to keep our parents out of hell. Something I would have to think about. Then I was blessed with her standing immediately in front of me with her enormous belly just inches from my head. She smelled a little bit like mildewed cabbage. I knew I could find her classroom in the dark.

Anyway, she stood there, her ruler held erect while attempting a conspiratorial smile and she said, "Here's what you do. When you're watching television, always leave right before the end of the program… or when you're eating dinner and have an especially good dessert, don't eat it."

Chapter 2 – Finding My Inner Alcoholic

Several of us actually groaned. She went on to say that our parents would eventually ask us why we are behaving this way and we could say that we were sacrificing to help them save their immortal souls and that they should get back to church. She didn't have a very good grasp of where I lived. My father was a Baptist, had his own Bible and didn't believe any of this crap, anyway. Going there filled no need I had ever perceived. I was just following orders. It did seem to make my mother happy, though. It did nothing for me.

After checking in the kitchen for anything edible, I went straight to my room and started taking off my ugly, brown, plaid, mothball smelling coat and gloves. I was still cold and not impressed by the gray and windy day outside. It was almost as gray and cold inside this tiny little room. Catechism was always a 50-50 shot at ruining my entire day. I felt funky. In my room, it was two steps from the door to my bed, if I didn't bump into the old door that was my desk and dresser. I wanted to kick something but I didn't have the energy. I heard my window rattle. I looked and there was a bare hand beating on the glass. It was Raymond, the strange kid that lived next door.

Raymond was not only strange but he was special. Not 'short school bus' kind of special, although he was probably just a blow to the head away from it. He held a place in my life that no one else would ever hold. He was my first drinking buddy. A person that, in my eyes, had opened doors for me into one of the joys of life. The very first time I had met him face-to-face was that past summer. I was sitting in my backyard on an old picnic table when he just walked over and sat down. He had one arm hanging down the side of him and he was holding something that I couldn't see it. He asked me if I liked beer and I said, "Sure." My beer drinking up to this point had been limited to a sip stolen from an adult's beer every six months or so. He looked around and then brought his arm up on the table with two bottles of Rheingold beer in his hand. He even had an opener. I started to like him. We drank the beers without speaking to each other. I had never had a full bottle of beer to myself.

Sober And Miserable

In about 15 minutes, I was seeing Raymond in a different light. Actually, the whole world had gotten quite a bit friendlier. It was an amazing moment. I can still remember every detail from that one beer. The smells in that corner of the yard filled me even though it was mostly cat piss because there was an old, broken down sandbox in the corner that nobody wanted to deal with.

At that very moment, it didn't bother me at all. I was with my buddy Raymond. It was also the first time I had ever peeled the paper label off a beer bottle. Even our dumpy little gray house sitting there 20 feet away felt comforting. It was a night of firsts. Raymond looked at me and said, "You know there's more?"

"What?" I said.

"There's more beer."

"Where?"

"Everywhere," he said with a big smile.

When I asked him what he meant, he almost giggled. He said he walked around the neighborhood a lot. I knew that and everyone in the neighborhood knew that. He had earned everyone's concern about his weirdness. On his walks, he would check out everyone's yard and driveway. He had discovered that many of these yards and porches had heavy cardboard boxes just sitting there. The tops opened from the center with flaps on three sides. When he got the courage to look inside, he found a treasury containing 24 beer bottles. That night's beer had come from this account. He said there were 20 or 25 of these just hanging around the neighborhood waiting to be taken. He got very serious and told me we could only take two from a case at a time. That way, they would probably never miss them if we just put the bottles back when we were done. So much for Raymond being retarded. Raymond was on his

Chapter 2 – Finding My Inner Alcoholic

way to being a friend. And not one I was willing to share. I was buzzed in so many different ways.

From that time on, we got together two or three times a week. He insisted on bringing the beer each time and had no complaint when I asked him to start bringing me two. A couple of times we shared my second beer and Ray got very talkative. He didn't show a lot of emotion but he did talk about how he missed his father. His parents had been divorced for a couple years. He said his house felt empty and was way too quiet with his father gone. His mother was sad and talked about moving back to Pennsylvania where she had family. This scared him. He said he was working on a building project in his room that he didn't want to leave. He said that more than anything else he would like a puppy for Christmas. That had been at the end of summer.

The weekend before school started, he caught me sitting alone on our front stoop. He asked me if I had ever been in his house. I said, "Of course not, you know that." He got a very serious look on his face and said this was the perfect time for a first visit.

We went to the backyard and into the house through the kitchen door, right into where his mother was doing dishes. She smiled and said, "You guys have a good time! Let me know if you need anything to drink or eat." I smiled back but didn't say anything because I was trying to keep up with Ray who was plowing ahead towards his room. I had also noticed how pretty she was, with long brown hair and a big smile. I was glad we had gone through the kitchen so quickly because I was probably blushing. Raymond had already gone down the hall and was waiting at his door. His hand was on the doorknob and he was actually jumping from foot to foot.

"Ready?" he asked.

"Coming, coming," I said.

Sober And Miserable

"You got to see this, man!"

I got to the door and he swung it open like it was door number three on The Price is Right TV show. He stepped inside his room and I was almost knocked over by a wall of odor more powerful than anything I had ever encountered, even in a public restroom. He slammed the door behind me and I was starting to wonder just what I had gotten into. The smell inside the room reminded me of the summer day our septic tank had to be pumped. My father thought it was funny when I puked. That is exactly how I felt at the moment when the door closed behind me.

I looked around for a wastebasket and didn't find one. It was the clothesbasket or the floor. The basket won. Strangely enough, it didn't seem to matter to Ray at all. He's just waved his hand at it as if it were no big deal. He was excitedly trying to show me the cage. The cage that took up half his room and went outside through a pane that had been removed from the window. It was made of bare lumber covered with chicken wire. The cage started about 2 feet off the floor and ran all the way to the ceiling. Inside the cage were two large, black squirrels and a maze of old tree branches. At the bottom of the cage, was the material that had been taken out of our septic tank. Well, it looked and smelled the same. He stood there with one arm extended almost as if he was saying, "Isn't this the most beautiful thing you've ever seen?" And in a lot of ways, I was truly amazed. Disgusted but amazed.

Raymond was living in this little room with 2 pounds of squirrel and 100 pounds of poop. I asked him if he had shown this room to a lot of people. Apparently, I was number one. Now, up to this point I thought I had the winner in the self-pity lottery by having to live in a three bedroom house with six other kids. Even when most of us were teenagers, our house never smelled this bad. Even after puking, I was starting to feel really bad for Raymond. I was looking at the little world he lived in. The stinky, little world he lived in. I asked him if his mother knew about the cage. He said, "Sure, she built it."

Chapter 2 – Finding My Inner Alcoholic

"Did you ask her to build it?"

"No," he said. "I was just letting squirrels come in through the hole in the window. She said it would be like a zoo."

"I've got an idea," I said. "Let's get a bucket and shovel out of the garage and clean this up. It might improve the smell in here."

I spent most of the afternoon shoveling poo with a little four-inch wide army surplus shovel. I would fill a bucket and Raymond would take it out and dump it in the back yard. If his mother noticed, she never said anything. We got the cage floor clean enough that we could see it was metal underneath. This really excited Raymond. He smiled and raced out of the room. He came back with what smelled like dirty bath towels. I asked him if he was sure if he wanted to do this and he said he was. So we polished up the floor of the cage until it was bright and shining. He was so proud of himself, he could hardly contain the joy. I grabbed him and told him we should go to the store.

"Why are we going to the store now?" he asked.

"For some finishing touches to your little zoo."

The pet store was about four blocks away and an easy carry for two 25-pound bags of cedar shavings. When we got back it took about a month of Sunday newspapers to cover the bottom of the cage. Lastly, Raymond spread 25 pounds of cedar shavings with great care, making sure every square inch was covered. With hands on his hips he marveled at his creation. And his room smelled a lot more like a forest than a sewage treatment plant. He was very quiet but he looked at me and asked if I could leave. I was a little bit surprised but he reached his hand out and touched me. He said it was ok, he just wanted to sit there alone and look at his cage. He was even a little strange when he was being nice.

Sober And Miserable

So, as I stood there in my cold bedroom, he was hitting the window harder and harder with his knuckles. My first thought was that it was too cold to drink beer outside. I really wished he would go away. When I scraped some of the ice off the inside of the window I could see that he was literally jumping up and down. His face was red and he was shouting something at me. Snot was flying everywhere and he looked really frightened. I wondered if he had finally gotten into some kind of trouble. I put my very old brown coat back on, took a right at the kitchen and went straight out the door. He was still jumping up and down when I got there. He kept telling me I had to help him. When I asked him what was going on, he just grabbed my sleeve and pulled me through the bushes. We went through his back door of the garage, slammed the door and stopped. The whole place smelled like dog poop.

"Did you get me over here to clean up another mess for you?" I asked.

"No, I just really need your help. I don't know what to do."

"You've only had this dog for a month. Not even. She was the only thing you wanted for Christmas. What the hell is going on?" I asked, a bit confused.

"She wouldn't stop pooping. It made me madder and madder every day. The same thing, pick up the dogs poop. Every day."

"Raymond, that's just part of having a dog."

"I've got a bigger problem than that now."

He grabbed the zipper of my coat then pulled me to the big front door of the garage. All I saw when I got there is a pile of dog poop about a foot across with a whole bunch of blood exactly in its center. I looked at Raymond and he didn't say anything. He broke my gaze when he turned his head to the right. My eyes followed his head and eyes as he

Chapter 2 – Finding My Inner Alcoholic

turned to look at something. At first, I couldn't tell what I was looking at. Then, the garage got very, very quiet. I actually couldn't hear anything. I thought I was looking at a black towel hooked to a chain that was thrown over the garage door track. Then I saw the dog's little pink tongue hanging from the side of his mouth. And blood was still dripping from the other end. I felt so cold. I couldn't think.

"No, no, God, no," kept swirling through my head. I couldn't believe this beautiful little Lab puppy was dead.

I turned to Raymond and he was standing there silently crying. I grabbed his shoulders and shook him so his head moved both back and forth.

"Raymond, what the fuck did you do?" I asked frantically.

"You've got to help me, you're the only one I have," he blubbered.

"How did this happen? What were you doing?"

"I came out here to pick up dog poop. She had pooped again all over the place. I was really, really angry and I started kicking her. She pooped again when I kicked her and I just started kicking her harder until she tried to run away. I tried to grab her but she just snapped at me. I wanted to teach her a lesson so I put the collar on her. I put her on her chain and threw it over the garage door track. The chain wasn't really long enough so I had to jump for it. When I did, her legs came up off the floor and she started choking. I tried to let the chain go but it was stuck on the track.

"So what did you do?"

"I came to get you."

"Jesus."

I just looked at him and felt like I had no idea who he really was. That poor dog was a sweet, little animal. Much sweeter than Raymond. I noticed that Raymond had blood on his hands and asked how it got there. He said that at first he didn't know what it was when it came of the dog so he touched it. I couldn't believe it but I knew he was telling the truth. I was feeling worse and worse by the minute and I just wanted to get out of there and away from him. He kept begging me to help him so he wouldn't get in trouble. I wanted to leave and walk away from him and hoped he got sent to reform school. But of all things, the picture of him walking into my yard with two bottles of beer opened a soft spot in my heart for him. I decided I would help him for a little while.

We had been standing there for a long time and it seemed like the snot was freezing on our faces. Being much taller than Raymond I reached up, unhooked the chain and laid the dog down on the floor. She was so little, it was hard to imagine anyone getting so angry with her. I made Raymond get two buckets and we started picking up dog poop. Raymond was astounded that it only took us two trips and about 20 minutes to get the garage all cleaned up. When we had finished that, we went over and stood by the puppy.

He looked at me and said, "What are you going to do with her?"

"YOU are going to bury her. And you're going to take her far away from our neighborhood to do it. After it gets dark you put her in a bag, take that old Army shovel and go by where they're building the new expressway and find a hole or dig one. And you'll go there alone and never tell anyone," I said.

He didn't say a word. He just nodded his head a tiny bit and for the 50th time wiped his snotty nose on his sleeve.

The warm friendly feelings that were developed for Raymond over that summer drained away pretty quickly. I guess my selfish motive for

Chapter 2 – Finding My Inner Alcoholic

helping him was to preserve my source of beer. I was so angry after he killed that dog that I realized I could steal the beer as easily alone as he could. And I wouldn't have to share. If I got caught I would only be responsible for myself. And I was never caught stealing the neighbor's beer over the next five years. This, unfortunately, gave me the idea that I was pretty slick.

Almost exactly 10 years later, I was on Christmas break from college. My mother told me that Raymond had been killed in Vietnam the week before. I hadn't even known he had joined the Army. Well, he was drafted. Without feelings of anger or harshness toward him, I had the strangest feeling that this was a good thing for him. At the service for him, they made him out to be a hero. The service was mercifully short with a priest who didn't even know him, giving the eulogy. I sat in the back of the chapel and finished off my half pint of bourbon. I wondered if Raymond had ever believed in God. I wondered if he did now.

Chapter 3

Homeward

That Saturday morning was hot and humid, much like any summer morning in the Ohio Valley. I sat on my wet balcony trying to read my morning meditation and put a good face on the day. Part of me appreciated how beautiful the day was, while a bigger part was more than a little bit concerned about the antsy feeling I had in my stomach. I was sober just a couple of days less than 10 months. Somehow, I thought I should be feeling better than I did. My home group meeting the night before had left me annoyed and I just wanted to get in the car and go. Self-righteous Bible thumpers have always irritated me. It's always about them anyway, not the Bible. The relentless pushing of the God thing and spirituality bothered me mightily. I wasn't sure what I believed. Or even if I even believed, at all.

My folks had just moved to Louisville that spring and now they were less than 100 miles away. I thought about driving up there but couldn't get excited about that idea either. Going to the noon meeting would only fill the hole between 12 and 1. This tiny little balcony was so very beautiful with newly green trees hanging directly over it, sharing their smells with every drop of moisture sliding from wet leaves. I sat there methodically tying my stomach in knots with non-problems. I got up, went out to my car, put the keys in the ignition and waited. I guess I was hoping for inspiration. I headed to I-75, knowing that in five minutes I'd have a choice of North or South. There was nobody I wanted to see North, and South would lead directly to my parent's home.

Chapter 3 – Homeward

Heading out of Cincinnati, the sun broke through the clouds making bright green patches bloom in the rolling pastures on either side of my car. I looked at that scene and knew that the gloom in my head needed some of that sunshine. The earthy smell of the farms and animals stirred the old, familiar feelings of being in Kentucky again. The chokehold I had on the steering wheel loosened just a bit.

I left the highway at Carrolton, about halfway there. The Kentucky River flowed into the Ohio here and I wanted to sit by the big river for just a minute. In college, I would come here to salve hangovers and broken relationships…and usually start a six pack. Today, the water was coffee brown and moving quite rapidly. I sat on an old bench among a tangle of trees at the water's edge. My shoulders dropped from my ears, easing up just being there again. Although the ground was damp, there was a freshness in that little spot by the river. I had always felt a sense of connection when I was here. I could take a deep breath and let my knotted up head relax. Even though I knew this water was nowhere near clean, my skin felt fresh and alive just sitting there.

Back in the 60s there was no interstate, just the old two lanes that followed the river's every twist and turn. Many a night, those twists let me know just how drunk I was as I tried driving back to campus. It was a fifty-mile gamble every time. It felt a little odd to be sitting there without a beer in my hand. I thought about all the times I sat there convincing myself that it was ok to have one or two. But, I never in my life bought one or two. It was like thinking about an old girlfriend that I finally accepted I wouldn't be seeing ever again. I noticed the sweat pouring down my back. It was time for me to leave my little shrine.

As the sun rose higher in the sky, the valley fog disappeared exposing a hundred different shades of green. The last 50 miles of this drive would be under a blazing sun. Even though I was physically much more relaxed, my mind started to scramble deciding what to say when asked why I was there. It would be simple enough to say, "I just wanted to see you all." But, I felt strange because I didn't really know why I was there. There just didn't seem to be anything special about this day. I was uncomfortable in my own skin and worried that I would make them a little nervous. My discomfort and restlessness had often preceded very unpleasant times.

As I drove towards home, the scenery became more dramatic. The road passed through great cuts of limestone rock and then opened into lush green pastures divided by traditional white board fences. There was a rhythm to this land that my body was starting to pick up. It was familiar and I felt comfortable there. Some of my antsyness was finally going away. I felt OK about just showing up at my parent's home. It's not that they are formal at all, they would be happy to see me. The discomfort was my own. Now, sitting in this beautiful countryside, I had a feeling deep in my stomach that I should be there. Something was pulling on me, I just didn't know what.

Being welcomed at home had not always been a sure thing for me. In the years before I got sober, there was always tension in the house when I arrived. There were still seven younger siblings at home. They might or might not acknowledge me. My mother would kiss me mainly to check my breath for alcohol. If my father managed to be in the house, he would nod and sometimes shake my hand. It's not that they were cold, they were warm and affectionate in most situations. Except, of course, when they were being gripped by the fear of impending doom that my visits seemed to bring. I frequently left behind disabled cars, hurt feelings, bruised egos and widespread disappointment...sometimes even a court date guaranteeing my reappearance. My father had been a county police officer for over 20 years and my adventures with the law brought brand new indignities to his life.

There was also the very tender issue surrounding my antics with women who I had brought home while I was in a blackout or thoroughly drunk. I found out the hard way that there is no way to sneak someone

Chapter 3 – Homeward

out of the house on a Sunday morning with nine people at the breakfast table. At least most of them thought it was funny. And no, that didn't include my parents. My mother did get a laugh when unidentifiable female underwear were found in the laundry. She folded them neatly and left them on my dresser. She also introduced me to humility when I thought I would raise hell about my little brother taking a nap in my bed and peeing in it. She pointed out that he had been at a friend's house for two days. I actually had to think about who it could have been until the obvious dawned on me. I still thought drinking was the only fun I had.

So, after less than 10 months in recovery, my family was happy just to see me walking in sober. Amazing rebound! I avoided letting them know I was coming, so they wouldn't cook anything or do anything special for me. I carried a lot of guilt and the attention there embarrassed me. I just wanted to walk in there and be one of the gang. I didn't want to be the one that needed attention, counseling, seeing the priest or Uncle Charlie. He was the family's very own alcoholic. People talked about him, too. It had been just about three years since my father and I had completely stopped speaking to each other. That was also the last time in our lives we had yelled at each other. But, there was a lot of yelling. My sister Kathy had returned to campus with me after Christmas break to get a taste of college life. Imagine a full-blown 60s experience including all the alcohol, drugs, romance and craziness that could be packed into a three or four day visit. I still don't know exactly what my sister did during that visit but I know she reported it to my father.

When I talked with him, he had the impression that I had exposed my sister to imminent death and debauchery. I suggested he had no appreciation of the 60s culture. He wholeheartedly agreed. He actually used words in that conversation that I had never before heard directed at me.

At one point, I thought he was going to read me my rights. I was quite mistaken. Actually, he didn't believe I had any rights. We finished with him saying, "You don't need to call here anymore," and I responded weakly with, "Fine". The time without talking seemed a lot longer in my head than it was on the calendar. I was painfully aware of this every time I wanted to speak with my father. This was when I learned what it was like to feel really alone...yet another fringe benefit of my drinking.

It was early afternoon by the time I got to their new house. This was a very pretty split-level that was much nicer than the house they had left behind in New York. The yard had kids and toys spread around and the garage my father had always wanted. He was there waving and smiling as I drove up, walking away from the lawnmower he had been working on, coming towards my car. He put his big, sweaty arm around me and invited me in for some lunch. This was definitely better than drinking. In that moment, I had a better high than I had ever experienced with any substance.

In the house, my mother was smiling and rattling dishes around for our lunch. I noticed that there was a dining room table and chairs that were brand new and a set of pewter candle holders in the middle of the table. My mother beamed with pride as she showed me the table. She had never before in her life had a dining room table or a dining room, for that matter. The candle holders were a gift from one of my aunts that she cherished for the rest of her life. For their entire lives, my mother and father had little more than the bare necessities for themselves. On every occasion, their eight children had come first. After the tiny three bedroom tract house in New York, this seemed like a palace. I was really surprised at how much a few little things made them happy.

The little house on Long Island was a happy place for our childhood. I hadn't felt deprived but I have realized recently how small that place was. It was tiny. Less than 700 square feet for everyone...three bedrooms, one bath and nine people all looking for a place to sit. The kitchen had no counter space and three small cabinets for food. The kitchen table was also the food prep area and the homework table and the place we

Chapter 3 – Homeward

went to "have a talk". I had a lot of the latter. It also served as the card table for a few kids, if we had company for dinner. The table didn't actually go in the kitchen. It went in the entrance by the front door where you could see into the kitchen and the front walk. It was considered a treat. We got a lot of mileage out of very simple things. My mother never drove a car. Most of the time, she walked to the grocery store. I never heard her complain. She always told me, "I'm a tough girl from Brooklyn…I can take care of myself."

We ate standing around in the kitchen, everyone pretty much chattering happily at the same time. My father finished first and slipped out the back door to finish his lawn mowing chores. The grass smelled good and everybody seemed to be in a great mood. The little kids, Lorraine, Nancy and Paul wanted me to go outside with them and go in the new swimming pool. It was a big above ground model probably 4-5 feet deep in the center. Although it was over 95° outside, the water in the pool felt like it was closer to 55°. I really wasn't very interested in getting in the pool with the kids. I wound up sitting down in the house with my mother who had brewed a pot of coffee just for the two of us. My mother was nearly crippled with rheumatoid arthritis and I really appreciated the little things she did for all of us.

She was always attentive to me when I was around, even during my drinking days. That particular day, she was the only one to ask me anything about my recovery. I told her that I was going to a lot of meetings and hanging out with my sponsor and his family. I wasn't dating anyone at this point but she wanted to hear about any girls I had even had coffee with. The coffee was her way of lubricating me and getting me to stay overnight. I told her I'd made a commitment to be at the eight o'clock meeting that night and to help clean up afterwards. I really didn't want to stay but I didn't want to hurt her feelings either. It was rolling past four o'clock and I was starting to think about leaving. If I left by five, I could be home by seven, cleaned up and at a meeting by eight.

Sober And Miserable

I was looking around for the little ones so I could say goodbye and be on my way. They had been having a great time jumping in the pool and running in and out of the house. This was accompanied by a lot of joyful squealing. I noticed the lawnmower had stopped running and I went looking for my father. I looked in front and back but he was nowhere to be seen. I went into the kitchen to ask if my mother had seen him. But she had not. About that time, Paul came in from the pool saying, "Dad won't play with me anymore and he's acting really weird."

"What's he doing?" I asked him.

"Just floating. Please come outside!"

My father was a big joker and I was sure he was just playing with Paul's head. I actually felt silly walking out the back door and calling for my father. But, there was no response at all. The ground was muddy and slippery from the pounding it got from the little kids. As I walked over to the pool, I noticed how quiet it was. No kids' voices, not even road noises. I was starting to get annoyed when I looked over the edge of the pool and saw my father floating face down in the center of the pool. I called to him, hoping that he was still playing a joke on us. But, he didn't look right and I was beginning to be overwhelmed by my thoughts and feelings. I remember thinking clearly, "God, I don't want to be here." I ran back into the house and grabbed my sister, Nancy. I told her to do exactly as I said and call 911, give them the address and tell them there had been a drowning.

I went back outside without talking to anyone on the way. Their faces all held a stunned look. Outside, I jumped into the pool and went over to my father. He was tinged blue and felt very cold. He weighed 275 pounds and I was starting to realize that I wasn't going to take him out of the pool on a little plastic ladder. I rolled him onto my shoulders and dragged him over the side of the pool onto the ground. He landed with a thud on his butt. I got out of the pool and rolled him onto his side, trying to clear his airway of any obstruction. I had taken the CPR course

Chapter 3 – Homeward

almost exactly 24 hours before I had to throw my father out of the pool and try to remember everything I needed to do.

I was shaking inside when I remembered trying to get out of the class. I even thought about just not going, dammit, it was at 3:30 on a Friday afternoon. When I put him on his back, I was crushed by the thought that he really looked like he was dead. I was so angry, I remember beating on his chest and yelling at him, "You can't do this, it's not fair, you've got to stay with us." I had done mouth-to-mouth for a little while and then started chest compressions. When I started chest compressions, a pink and foamy discharge came out of his mouth. It looked like it was pieces of his lung floating in the foam. This little observation did nothing for my confidence. Fortunately, I was way too scared to stop. After several minutes, he coughed and was trying to take breaths on his own. He had still not regained consciousness when the paramedics arrived. I rode in the ambulance with the paramedics and could tell that they were not optimistic about my father's future. They took us to University Hospital and put him in the 1971 version of a trauma room.

I was left in the waiting room in soaking wet shorts, t-shirt bare feet… and I was alone. After about half an hour sitting there, I started to shake violently until a nurse came over and gave me a sweatshirt. As I started to warm up, my senses started coming back. It seemed like all I had seen for the past two hours was my father's naked chest and my fists pounding on it. For that time, that's all there was in my world. After I got done yelling at him, I decided that I wouldn't stop CPR until he started breathing again. That's all there was. No sounds, no pictures and no time. Just me and him. I tried to remember who was at the house but could only remember the little kids. And I was pretty sure they didn't drive. I was looking for a phone when I realized it was a new house and I didn't even know the phone number.

One of the nurses must have noticed that I was about to cry and came over to me and asked what I needed. When I told her I needed a phone number, she told me to wait a minute. In less than a minute, she was back with the phone number from the paramedics report. I was astonished. It felt like a miracle had occurred right in front of me. I called home to talk with my mother and she and everyone else was surprised to find out that dad was still alive. There was a lot of yelling and crying. I told her that he was in a coma and could be for quite a while. He also had aspiration pneumonia from the water he had taken into his lungs. Just about that time, I was told he was being taken up to ICU.

My Uncle Jerry finally came to the hospital to pick me up. I had been there about seven hours but it seemed like minutes. Mostly, I prayed that God would spare this good man who had worked so hard during his life. From time to time, I tried to bargain with God offering myself as substitution if he would let my father live. I finally gave up praying. I thought about the meeting that I would have been in had I not been here. I remembered them telling me at every meeting to 'Just trust God'. I thought I could. I also knew I had no better choice available. So much of this program is like that.

As I got to the front door at my folks house, I was still wearing wet pants. At least I hadn't peed in them. The finishing touch came later by my uncle Roush. He was holding the front door open, wearing a great big smile and holding a giant tumbler full of scotch. He said, "Time for you to relax, you've had a big day."

I had to laugh! My life had turned on a dime and now I had the opportunity to dissolve the entire thing with 6 ounces of scotch whiskey. I gave uncle Rouse a hug and went on into the house. When they saw me, my sisters started crying again and I joined right in. The most upset was the youngest, Paul. He was literally wringing his hands and I could see the fear in his eyes. I put my arms around him and tried as hard as I could be sincere when I wasn't sure of anything. I told him that dad would be alright and I could feel his body relax. I hoped he would sleep that night.

Chapter 4

Confusion

I am sober 12 years now and my dreams are starting to come true. Sort of. I have a very pretty wife, a precious daughter and the beautiful Maine woods on all four sides. It is a short walk down to the Penobscot River. The outsides are all looking pretty good. And on the inside we have a new baby coming soon. In spite of all of this, I am still very unsettled and shaky inside. Around the house, I go from one project to the next, seldom completing any of them. I have all the material fruits of sobriety and I still get no feeling of satisfaction. It is confusing to have all this and still want more. Every woman I see is a temptation in one way or another. Every project I am involved with, displays opportunities for me to get involved with mischief. I somehow have a gift of being able to see every unscrupulous way that money can be made. And I rarely appreciate the risk. Consequences, including the loss of my freedom, never penetrated my consciousness in any meaningful way. I somehow developed a way of thinking that traded off my good behavior of sobriety for my bad behavior of a generally amoral approach to life. Unless I was involved in some kind of "action", I was gloomy and unmotivated.

On March 1, in a screaming Maine blizzard, my son Eric was born at home. We lived 8 miles out in the country and had planned a home delivery all along. Unfortunately, we didn't plan for it to be that night. My wife was at full term but had had no signs of impending labor. Being the dutiful husband, I decided to go to town for a meeting. There was only light snow falling and I was bored. I dressed my boredom up as a desire to help a friend who was going through a rough time. I actually hoped that I wouldn't run into him at the meeting. He was there and hurting so we went for a cup of coffee. In 1982, there were no cell phones but I did have a beeper. When I got to talk to my wife on the phone, she was somewhat excited. Seems that somewhere in the eight miles between where I was and where she was, a very different snowstorm had come in. I thought she was out of breath from running for the phone. But, in fact, she'd gone into labor. And according to her it was moving along very quickly. I actually considered waiting awhile and calling her back to see if she was really in labor.

When I got to my driveway it was nearly 10 o'clock and six inches of snow had fallen. The only marks in the snow were from my neighbor, Kathy, as she ran to my house. I really wasn't relishing going in the house. We were supposed to have a doctor there but I could see that his car was not in the driveway. This signaled my stomach to begin to churn. I really wanted to run away. When I walked through the front door, Kathy, our neighbor, locked on me with huge eyes and a slightly crazed smile. She said, "Come on, we have a baby to deliver!"

"Can't you do that?" I asked.

She rolled her eyes and started walking towards the bedroom. I followed and walked into the bedroom to be greeted by a sweaty, angry, naked woman who looked a little bit like my wife. She asked me what the fuck I was thinking being out so late? I didn't think it was a good time for a strictly honest reply. I held my tongue and looked around the room trying to get a clue of what I was supposed to do. Her contractions were less than two minutes apart when I'd walked into the room. And both women were telling me to "catch the baby".

Now, to my blood deprived brain, I had visions of a baby suddenly shooting out from between her legs. I did actually know better than this

Chapter 4 – Confusion

but I couldn't get my brain to grasp what was happening. The inside of my head kept shouting, "Where is that damn doctor?"

About then, my wife stiffened up and said, "Come over here!"

I looked down and thought I could see the baby's head beginning its exit. As I had visions of this baby shooting out at me, I was starting to accept that I might have to deliver this baby. Right then, at 10:35PM, Bill, our doctor tromped into the room spraying snow everywhere. He was all happy and bubbly. I thought he might be drunk. But he wasn't and when he looked at my wife, he realized he had better get to work. Five minutes later my son Eric joined the world. 90 minutes later, the house was quiet, mother and baby asleep and daddy cleaning up the mess. At about 2AM my wife woke up and yelled for me and scared me silly. When I got back to the room, she seemed very confused and wanted to know what I had done with the placenta. Without hesitation I told her I had fed it to the dog. She looked at me and said, "You're such an asshole!" And went right back to sleep. The dog had really liked it.

This experience was harder on me than our first child's birth. Probably because I was 500 miles away when that blessed event took place. I got to the hospital a couple of hours after the delivery so everybody was cleaned up and in their proper place. I hadn't been able to get a flight from Chicago to Michigan so I had to drive. That day was a crystal-clear, warm, blue sky kind of day. I spent nearly two hours with my new daughter Becky and her cranky mother. I'd gotten there as fast as I could but she wasn't actually all that excited about seeing me. Our relationship had grown quite chilly during her pregnancy. It could be that the little discussion we had at the beginning of her pregnancy might have affected her mood and attitude toward me. I had been at an AA retreat for the weekend and had a brilliant insight that she was to blame for my chronic unhappiness. After all, I was working a good program and generally doing everything right. I never really considered any other option as a source for my negative take on life's less than joyful moments.

Sober And Miserable

When I got home on Sunday afternoon, it was a lovely fall day, dry and crisply cool. She was there waiting for me with a smile and a kiss. I even recall thinking how her timing was, as usual, a little off.

I announced that I needed to talk. I felt like I was being sufficiently ominous but she just wasn't getting it. We had been married about two and a half years at this point. The relationship stumbled between fights full of my rage, her stubbornness and both of us needing to be right. I was ready to give up. I had figured out that what I really needed was to be free of this woman. My plan was to tell her as soon as I could after getting home that I was leaving. We would get divorced. I had spent the weekend convincing myself, and the men I was with, that I was the victim in this relationship. I had done what I thought I needed to do to make sure I wouldn't be looked at as a bad person. I can honestly say that I never once in this process thought about what this would do to my wife. I had convinced myself that she was the guilty party.

We sat there crying quietly and she said, "I have something I need to talk about, as well. I found out yesterday that I am pregnant."

If she hadn't been crying, I would've thought she was making it up to hurt me. I was so angry because I thought I had been tricked. I was angry because I didn't think I had the courage to divorce her anyway. I was absolutely correct. I was far too concerned about how I would appear in the community. Then, I was afraid that she would want to get divorced anyway and ruin me in the community. I was totally deflated. I wanted to go to a meeting if only to get out of there. And I did. I got up, left her there and went to a meeting. And I talked about God and gratitude and how the program had restored my integrity.

That evening, after Becky was born, I was leaving the hospital to go home when a nurse called out to me and asked me if I had had dinner yet. I had always found this particular nurse to be quite attractive. She invited me to have dinner at her house. The thought of the dinner and

Chapter 4 – Confusion

what may follow was absolutely intoxicating. And I knew I couldn't do it. Only because I was afraid of getting caught in this very small town we lived in. I was so disgusted with myself that I hardly slept that night. I was caught in the dilemma I created by wanting to do something I knew was wrong on one hand and feeling cheated on the other because I could not summon the balls to do it anyway. I slept that night just to get away from myself.

After her pregnancy with Becky, our relationship never fully recovered. Regardless of the season, there was always a chill in the air. For the next fourteen years, we limped along from one wound and to the next. We endured separations that lasted from weeks to months. We would blame each other for imagined wrongs and never really establish a bond that could hold us together. I believe we tried the best we could under the circumstances. Those circumstances were such that I always had to be right when there was a difference of opinion. I was not yet in touch with the damage being done by my own blind, self-centeredness. In meetings I spoke about God, yet had no personal contact with Him. I was an AA academic. My outside appearance had improved but inside I was as troubled and lost as I had ever been. I had blind spots that could block out the sun. I truly didn't know what I didn't know. And I was so wrapped up in myself that I was not interested in having someone point out my shortcomings, regardless of how much it might have helped. While I didn't drink or use other substances during this time period, my alcoholism still steadfastly kept me from forming healthy relationships. I desperately wanted the contact of human intimacy. But, I was too sick to see it sitting right in front of me.

Chapter 5

The Pitch Men

If I had acquired any wisdom at all in the pursuit of recovery from alcoholism, little or none of it had been self-generated. It usually came from the wise men around me. In the early 1990s, I had moved to Providence, Rhode Island to take a crappy job that looked good at the time. The job only looked really good in light of the fact that I didn't have one at the time. My divorce was final and so was my old job. And now I was going to be 300 miles away from my children. It would take a lot of work for me to see this move to Providence as a good thing. I knew in my heart I was just there for the job. With this very marginal attitude, I was an easy target for this group of sober men that became known as "The Pitch Men".

I spent my first weekend in Providence moving into a really nice apartment in the College Hill neighborhood. I was steps from Brown University and lived in the middle of homes and apartments dating as far back as the early 1700s. It was February, cold and damp. I was done unpacking by late afternoon and had time to go to a very trendy, buy-one-pay-double grocery store a couple of blocks away. That's when the full weight of my aloneness set in. I stood there in the bright, butcher-block kitchen and thought, "Okay, what do I do now?"

I missed my kids. That feeling had chased me around all weekend. It was catching up. I needed to do something. I didn't want to wind up sitting in a corner crying before I had curtains on the windows. I knew

Chapter 5 – The Pitch Men

there was a meeting on the street that I lived on at 7 o'clock. I didn't want to go. I was afraid. I didn't want to start over again in a new place. I had moved many times in my recovery. I was tired. My ego told me I was weary. At 6:30pm, I locked the door behind me and went looking for the Unitarian Universalist Church.

Everyone was friendly and welcoming. Of course. They always were. The bastards. Twenty-five hardy souls on this winter night came out of their warm homes to sit through a meeting of a group called "Breathing Easy". A non-smoking meeting was quite a rarity at the time. The group ranged from young Brown students to elder statesmen. They all smiled and reached out to me. Many gave me phone numbers and urged me to call if I needed anything. One man, in his early 70s, held back a bit after the meeting and waited until I was alone to introduce himself. He told me his name was Ned and had a broad smile and a strong handshake. He said he lived in Boston and Providence and would be happy to show me around the meeting scene in town.

As we walked out into the parking lot, he pointed down the street and told me about the meeting he would be at tomorrow afternoon at 5:30pm. It was right in the middle of the Brown campus and about three blocks from where we stood. The name of the meeting was "The Common Bond". I said I would meet him there the following day. The "Bond" would soon become my home group.

I have little recollection of my first day on the new job. I did have the impression that a lot of people were treading lightly. Later I found out that I have not been the boss's first choice. And, he was the one who told me. Working there was so stressful and unpleasant that I felt like I couldn't breathe until I left in the afternoon. The organization was an ego driven madhouse. Self-aggrandizement and political positioning was everyone's first order of business. There is no exaggeration in saying that the AA meetings I went to after work were my refuge. Walking into that meeting after work felt just like coming home to a child who had been lost. Acceptance hung in the air like Jasmine on a warm night. The energy of fellowship was a palpable substance.

On that first Monday night that I went to the Common Bond, Ned was standing out front in the cold, smiling broadly when he saw me. His gloved hands held two large steaming cups of coffee from Peaberries, our local coffee shop. It was blissfully pre-Starbucks. I took my coffee from his hand and we went up the granite steps into a beautiful Greek revival classroom building. More often than not, AA meetings were held in damp, church basements and you sat on cold metal chairs. The "Bond", as it was called by locals, was in an aboveground, carpeted meeting room with comfortable chairs and 15-foot high windows. This group was heavily populated with students, artists and intellectuals. Providence was a very artsy town. The mix made for a very interesting approach to recovery. Half the group was sober only for weeks, the other half had more than 10 years. Everyone dressed well. Everyone was friendly. I liked it and I didn't want to leave.

After the meeting was over, Ned introduced me to Dave and John. Twenty years later Dave and John are still close friends of mine. That night, Ned suggested we get a bite to eat. We found a hole in the wall Thai place on Meeting Street. I immediately enjoyed Dave's wit and dry, but upbeat, way of looking at everything. He was about my age, quite a bit shorter and about the same weight. He also had a full head of hair and a full face of hair. He worked in the family dish business at the other end of the state. In Rhode Island, that means it was about 30 minutes away.

John, by contrast, was very quiet and at our initial meeting, seemed to be painfully shy. As I got to know him, I realized he was fairly new to recovery. He was also an Ivy League educated lawyer who was currently working as a night watchman. John was a sensitive and very articulate man. He spoke as engagingly as any professor I had ever had in college. He was a voracious reader and had developed a taste in music that ran

Chapter 5 – The Pitch Men

from the ordinary to classical opera. As shy as he was most of the time, I learned that John was fundamentally a person driven by deep compassion. In his own way, he taught me a great deal. After dinner that night, we agreed we would all come to the meeting again next Monday and get dinner again.

The following week, I got to meet Bill and Peter after the meeting when they joined us for dinner. Bill was sober a long time and in his early 60s when we met. Another smiler, he was still able to walk into a room and light it up. He has spent most of his life working with his hands, and although he was getting old for that kind of work, he was still in demand because of his skill and trustworthiness. He said he lived in Newport because that's where the most people had money and couldn't do anything for themselves. He also possessed an incisive mind and an ability to cut through the fluff and pretense in AA and Newport alike. While he appeared to most people to be dignified and a bit standoffish, those close to him knew his raucous laugh and sense of humor. He would challenge me and comfort me. Peter was another handsome man with many years of recovery behind him. He was a successful contractor and builder in southern Rhode Island. I knew that within 15 minutes of meeting him. He also played the cello. Peter was the only one of the gang that I didn't connect with immediately. I judged his ego to be too large and heart too small.

At one of our Monday evening dinner sessions, the subject of cooking came up. We were all fairly quick to admit that we were talented, if not gifted, at meal preparation. After ample time allowed for bragging, we all seemed to arrive at the conclusion that we should be cooking for ourselves…and saving tons of money to boot.

A month passed and everyone showed up in my apartment for dinner after the meeting. It was a nice arrangement, the host preparing the entrée and the other guys splitting up the salad, beverage, bread and dessert. I made the heaviest chili I could prepare and the crowd was well pleased. We sat around patting our bellies, proud of our great creativity for entertainment. There was almost never talk of AA. We were much happier gossiping and bragging about our lives or our planned lives. Lively criticism of each other's weight, clothing and choice of women was the norm. Nobody ever left one of these dinners unscathed. And only on the most rare occasion did anyone leave angrily. Actually, that didn't happen until we started playing cards. The game was called "pitch" and while no gambling was involved, one's ego was always at risk.

Adding a game of chance to our regular dinner made the evening long enough that we had to change nights or find a different group. We moved our night to Thursday. For five years, Thursday nights were the high point of my week. The food part got a little competitive and we all gained weight. During this time, Peter, John, David and I changed residences at least once. The game went on. The game is a simple one. It is also called "high – low – Jack" to indicate the cards you would score points for having at the end of the hand. I think. I did not excel at this particular game. Each week, I was greeted with some unsubtle derision such as "Masters degree is here. Anyone have any questions?" Fortunately, I was not the only one subjected to the group's wit. I did have an unbroken record of many years without a win. I like to say I lost with distinction but it was actually bewilderment. The game was too simple for me to master, I just had to complicate it. Nothing new there.

While we were supposed to rotate locations each week, the summers provided a challenge.

Dave's place was a very rustic three-room cottage that backed up to the ocean in South Dartmouth, Massachusetts. It had a bedroom on either end and a little kitchen/dining area right in the middle. No electricity. Propane for gas lighting and the refrigerator needed to be turned upside down periodically to keep it working. The path to the outhouse was pure white sand. It was a two-holer but I had never heard of both seats being occupied at the same time. The view from the throne

Chapter 5 – The Pitch Men

was a beautiful stretch of the Atlantic Ocean. It was never stinky. The outhouse, I mean. Well, unless you were inside. The shower was a pipe hanging off the northeast corner of the building. It was not an enclosed shower. It tested many a person's modesty. Given our ages and food consumption, ogling was extremely rare and unrewarding. In spite of what city dwellers may have considered shortcomings in the cottage, we knew it was heaven on earth.

While finishing another sumptuous dinner on the beach and lingering over dessert and coffee, Dave piped up, "Peter, are we going to see you Monday at the Bond?"

"You keeping track of my meetings now?" Peter asked.

"Nothing much to keep track of lately."

"I could ask you what business it is of yours…"

"Peter, your mental health is my business."

"How's that?"

"By default, when you're not paying any attention to it."

"Maybe I like being a little crazy."

"Do you like being a little drunk?"

"Not lately."

"So what's going on? Seems like you might be drifting away."

"Not drifting. Maybe running. I'm tired of all the pretentious, sanctimonious bastards at that meeting."

"Peter, I'm hurt."

"I am just not getting anything out of it. Twenty years of hearing the same shit over and over again has worn me out. It's the first year over and over again."

"Just say for a minute that you are correct. We all know that you are too effin' crazy to go it alone."

"What do you think I'm doing here?"

"Eating my food and annoying us the rest of the time!"

"It's about time we got serious and started playing cards."

The discussion of how and why we stayed sober after 20 or more years was woven into everything we did. Half of us were usually troubled by the thought and the others were sure they had the solution. The halves varied greatly as to composition. No matter which side we took, the true comfort came from taking that position with each other. Was AA our lifeboat? That debate was unanswerable. Eventually we acknowledged that it was there but we were still deeply troubled about what to do with our time in the lifeboat. It seemed we all needed some kind of mission in life.

A couple of years after the conversation mentioned above, Peter was diagnosed with a serious form of cancer. Almost immediately after his surgery, he joined us for dinner and cards at Ned's house. He was still in obvious pain and wearing surgical dressings. He immediately made it clear that this is where he wanted to be. Not at an AA meeting but with a bunch of cranky old guys. I remember him smiling and grimacing as he sat down at the dinner table and said, "Alright you guys, shut up and deal!" We just figured it had been weeks since Peter had been in a position to irritate anyone. Inexplicably, he won very often. And we didn't

Chapter 5 – The Pitch Men

play for money, only the much more serious reward of bragging rights. He was back in his element.

Shortly before I left Rhode Island to move to Florida, Peter and I had lunch. I liked Peter and wanted to say a proper goodbye and thank him for all his help. Emotionally generous person that I am, I asked him if he had just stopped going to AA meetings. He said that he went occasionally and that he was very happy now that he was married and had an active family life. We are socially trained in AA to be cynical about people who don't go to very many meetings or to regular meetings. But, here sitting in front of me, was a man who's eyes shone and body relaxed when he talked about his wife and his family. He had found a venue to be loving and kind and was full of joy. And he was still sober. To say nothing of the gratitude he shared just by his joyful way of living. I believe the family was his church. I believe he professed his faith every day by loving his wife and children openly. This man that I hadn't liked very much six years before, had taught me by demonstration that I wasn't much of a judge of character. He made a beautiful thing out of his life by finding the place where he could love openly.

David was a different story altogether. I felt like I bonded with him the first time we went out to dinner in that little Thai place on Meeting Street near Brown University. There was as much ease and comfort in the relationship then, as there is now, over 20 years later. We've enjoyed the high sailing on the ocean in a small sailboat and shared the despair of romantic relationships that failed. In the mid-90s, Dave and his wife lived in downtown Newport on Thames Street. Their house was an old, gray three-story tenement whose upper two floors overlooked Newport Harbor. The first floors were businesses and the whole place was generally warm and funky. It was usually filled with warm and funky people. During holiday season each year, they lived there they put on a much-anticipated Christmas party. It was big doings on Thames Street. Most of the artsy and creative community showed up. I don't know if the butcher and baker with there, but there were several candlestick makers…and jewelry makers. Craftspeople galore. It was about 10PM and the party was going strong with new food offerings arriving every few minutes. My favorite part of the holidays! As I was ogling the dessert table, Dave asked if I would come outside for a minute.

We started walking away from downtown Newport toward the end of the street that was definitely darker and quieter. I noticed during the evening that Dave had been a little bit more serious than he usually was but didn't appear to be very unhappy. Once again my intuitive skills failed me. After we had walked a few minutes, I started to notice how cold it was. I was also getting uncomfortable with the silence.

"What's going on, Dave?" I asked.

"I think she's gonna leave me," he said.

"Come on, you two get along great."

"We do, actually we are still good friends."

"Then, what's going on?"

"I'm not sure but I think there's someone else."

"Get out!"

"Last night she said she might need to get away for a while. She talked very softly like she was talking to a child. It was almost as if she was already gone. I don't know what I'm going to do."

"I will be here for you for whatever you need."

"What I need right now is for her to stay. I'm just sad. I can't think about anything else."

Chapter 5 – The Pitch Men

"Have you told her you want her to stay?"

"Yeah, she just looked away and wouldn't make eye contact with me."

"Dave, we will get through this whether she goes or stays."

"I just don't know."

I wanted to do something to make him feel better. I got along with his wife but had no illusions about being close to her. There was no way I could influence her and felt I probably shouldn't try. He would suffer mightily for many months after she left. In the end, his near-perfect acceptance of the situation led to peace for him. We spent a lot of time together going to meetings and movies and just hanging out at the beach. I was impressed with the grace he embodied as he went through this most difficult time. Less than six months later, I was in the same situation that he had been in. One evening after cards, it was just the two of us left and he put his feet up and smiled.

"I guess it's time for payback, huh?" he said.

"What?" I said, thinking I had screwed something up while playing cards. I was kind of out of it.

"No, I just want to let you know I'm here for you as you go through this nasty time with Marina."

"Maybe you should borrow my gun and just shoot me."

"No way! You made a point of keeping me off bridges during my divorce, why would I let you off so easily?"

"So, am I hearing this right? You want to watch me suffer?"

"Is there something wrong with that?"

"You are a mean little bastard."

"I'm not so little. And my parents got married a week before I was born."

"You're still mean."

"Is there a point to this?"

"When does the support come in?"

"When you pull your head out of your ass and start acting like a big boy."

"You're cold, too."

"Thank you!"

"How do I know when I'm getting better?"

"You will think it happens when you start entertaining ideas about another woman. But you will be wrong. You need to stay away from women for a year or two."

"You've got to be kidding! I just realized that you want me out on the competition for women!"

"You are truly a mental case! We should probably find a shrink and go to couples counseling."

"I know I'm crazy. Why you?"

Chapter 5 – The Pitch Men

"Because I'm here sitting talking with you and listening to you!"

For the next several months, I had a key to Dave's place at the beach and we spent so much time together, the gay couple down the road started inviting us to their parties. Dave thought it was hilarious and it just pissed me off. He thought that was pretty funny, too. For nearly 90 days and 90 nights, I had somebody I could talk with whom I trusted. By the end the summer, I had a nice tan, had been able to stop obsessing over that woman, and become deeply appreciative of Dave's simple lifestyle at the beach. His simple act of kindness by sharing his home and patient ear had begun to restore me to a form of sanity. Although he told our gay friends that we were straight they always winked at us when they walked by on the beach. Dave and I both had new girlfriends by Christmas.

John had asked me to be his sponsor a couple of months after we must first met. I was surprised and flattered. John was much smarter than me and much better educated. I was intimidated and didn't know if I could help him. He was a very charming, handsome and articulate Irishman from a prominent Rhode Island family. John had almost everything. That is, except a solid grasp on reality. This feature of his personality also scared the hell out of me. Right here, I have to point out a belief or bias I have about every alcoholic. We are all nuts. All of us! While many of us will deny it vociferously, I believe we are all affected more or less by mental illness. For some of us, the mental illness is more prominent than the alcoholism. Most of us though, have to stop drinking before we get a good grasp on just how crazy we are. Everyone I know in recovery, has either had some therapy and treatment or they are still struggling with demons. At that time, John had an extended family of demons living with him.

John worked with unusual dedication to get his balance back. While his progress wasn't meteoric, it was steady. In that first year that I knew

John, most people simply characterized him as being a very shy and private man. That was exactly how he appeared in social situations.

What people couldn't see was the pain John suffered from not being able to communicate the way he desired. Whenever John and I got together for coffee or a meal, he had genuine interest in how I was feeling. He was always glad to see me. For all of his challenges, John worked his heart out. He was always focused on being there for his children. Through all of his troubles, he maintained daily focus on being a good father.

My relationship with John allowed me to become grateful for the experience of knowing him. As John regained his confidence it was immensely rewarding for me every time he had a small victory. After a few years of recovery, he had returned to the practice of law. While he still wasn't excited about dealing with the public at large, he developed a niche serving other lawyers. He got to the point of writing appellate briefs on major cases for serious trial lawyers. I probably overdid it but I couldn't stop telling him how proud I was of him. He would smile, his face would turn red and he would say, "It's just my job, Dale." John being John, taught me a great deal about dignity. Once we were talking about God and he said he really only needed to know one thing, that there was one, and it wasn't him. He was happy with that, it suited him. He's been one of my biggest instructors in humility. He looked at being humble before his God, as an asset, not a liability.

Ned, although appearing genteel and laid-back can be surprisingly coarse and abrasive. When my relationship with Marina broke up, he went on a mission. I thought it was just going to be dinner and some consolation.

"You're an idiot," he said softly, but not gently.

"Excuse me?" I asked.

"How could you possibly let her go?"

Chapter 5 – The Pitch Men

"In the end, it was surprisingly easy."

"Jesus, you are a fool."

"I take it that you don't approve?"

"She's a goddess."

"Did you get here early and start drinking again?"

"No, why can't you see that she was a trophy."

"Oh yeah! She's beautiful, a successful doctor and a crazy Cuban woman. Perfect material for a soap opera."

"They're all crazy."

"This is a product of your past experience with women?"

"Well, I am older and much more experienced than you are!"

"I thought you were only married once."

"Twice."

"My mistake."

"No, mine. I should've done it six or seven times."

"You couldn't have afforded more than another two or three." I jabbed.

"Hmmm, you're probably right. Economics does determine quantity. But you had that covered with Marina. You screwed up."

Sober And Miserable

"Would you like an introduction? I happen to know she's available. Too bad she's an internist and not a proctologist."

"She definitely was beautiful. When you got the new pool, I was hoping to get an invite to the pool party."

"We didn't have a pool party. We were busy hating each other and sulking. And you've told me 100 times that you don't like swimming in a pool."

"My fantasy was that I would get to see her naked."

"Why didn't you just ask her?"

"You mean she would've shown me?"

"Not in a million years, crazy man."

"Why are you so mean to your friends."

"It's the little things in life that make it worth living."

"I was going to buy dinner, too!"

"Sure you were. Right after the second coming."

And we walked out of the cozy little restaurant in downtown Providence with Ned's arm draped across my shoulders. He smiled all the way to the parking lot wagging his finger at me for my poor choice of relationship moves. The whole evening was silly as could be. Somehow I walked out of there feeling 100 pounds lighter and knowing Ned would always be my friend.

They were four guys who changed me more profoundly with their simple, open and loving style more than 10,000 egomaniacs telling

Chapter 5 – The Pitch Men

me how to live. They shared their trust and their lives with me as they unfolded their days. They had great stories but they weren't their stories. They all lived in the present no matter how difficult the task was. They lived with great dignity and humility. They really lived. They didn't spend their lives just talking about living. Each one of them in their own way showed me that life could be lived to its fullest without meeting the demands of conventional wisdom. I am forever grateful to them all.

Chapter 6

This Little Piggy

Living in Lebanon, New Hampshire was a pleasure in almost every way. It is a beautiful little community in the upper Connecticut River Valley. Every season is a treasure for the senses. In the mid 1980s it was close knit, genuine, and caring. I guess, if you like 120 inches of snow a year, it was perfect. The town even ran a little rope tow ski area for the kids, free of charge. Our house was a comfy two-story colonial sitting on 7 acres just five minutes from town. The gentle hills of the town produced great views year-round and truly interesting driving in the winter. The only AA meetings in town happened to be in the hospital where I worked. So, I went to meetings in Hanover just 5 miles up the road.

Of all the places I've lived before and after, the Upper Valley was by far the best. There was great beauty in the geography and the people. The only possible drawback was a predictably harsh winter. But it was easy to see how the snow and crystal clear nights had their own special qualities. The people that lived there were gentle and kind. They smiled even when it was 10 below. The town still had a town square with beautiful colonial homes laced throughout the village. Aside from the endemic curse of domestic violence, there was virtually no criminal activity. It was a grand place to raise children. Shortly after moving to Lebanon, we met two of these gentle and kind people, Janet and John.

Janet worked at the same hospital that I worked at. She and John had come from Boston looking for a place to raise her two boys that was not

Chapter 6 – This Little Piggy

such a struggle. They had a little farm about 25 miles out of town. They built a simple but elegant log home beside a creek deep in the woods. The first time we went out there, our kids fell in love with the place. There was so much to do! One field had a half dozen sheep and an equal number of lambs. I can still see Becky and Eric chasing those lambs. Twenty feet in front of their main door was a lined pond filled with trout.

The pond served many purposes. In the summer, it was a swimming hole and in the winter it was a skating rink. All year-round, it was a vital source for water, should a fire start. When John came out to feed his trout, I thought Eric was going in the pond when he saw all those fish come to the surface. He couldn't contain the joy! The kids played so hard that day that they were asleep before we made it back to the main road on our way home.

Whenever we were all together during the next week, the subject would always come around to the animals Janet and John raised on the little farm. Beside the sheep and lambs there were pigs, chickens and a couple cows. Becky quickly figured out how to divide our five-acre backyard to have room for her own menagerie. She put the pigpen in the far corner, the henhouse right in the middle where there was a shed containing my lawnmower and gardening equipment. The rabbits would go right behind the garage. When her mother wasn't complaining, I sensed the beginning of a conspiracy. I pointed out that I had a full-time job and wouldn't be much help. Uncharitably they said they knew that. The battle was over when their mother said they would invite Janet and John over to discuss pigs and chickens.

Don't let me give you the impression that everything was perfect. After almost 10 years of marriage, Wendy and I still had not figured out how to be happy with each other. For me, saving grace was in having someone to blame for my misery. I was clueless on the subject of responsibility. I still labored under the illusion that my feelings came from other people's actions. I was a main contributor to the illusion that

Sober And Miserable

I was powerless. I had ceded authority over my feelings to anyone who might step on my toes or bat their eyes at me. This was a nearly ideal community to live in but it was as if I was looking at a beautiful tank full of fish. I was clearly on the outside looking in.

Janet and John did come out the next weekend for a lovely dinner. And we were treated to the addresses and phone numbers of the local pig and chicken purveyors. We were given pamphlets, manuals and books on every aspect of small-scale ranching. Becky was ecstatic. She didn't even want to wait until spring. But Janet assured her that was the only practical course. Pigs first in early April, and chicks in mid to late May. Becky and Janet retreated to the family room to discuss the fine points of building a pigpen. I vaguely heard the discussion between them turn to sheep. This time, Becky came back into the kitchen with one index finger raised I caught her before she could say a single word and I said, "No sheep, absolutely no sheep." She stomped her foot and left the kitchen. This may have been the only fight she lost when it came to the animals. And I was already thinking about buying a new truck. It would be a "work truck". Ah, sweet justification.

It was a very cold day in early April when we went out to Grafton to pick up our own little piglets. Becky, of course, went with me to make sure I did it right. She was even determined to ride in the bed of the truck as we brought the pigs home. Everybody already knew how much I loved Becky, so there was nothing she could do to ride in the bed of the pickup. The little pink babies made it home just fine. I had set up a little pen about 4' x 4' in the corner of the garage as a home until the weather warmed up a bit. It was immediately clear that Becky didn't approve of this arrangement. "Dad, you can't leave them alone out here!" she said.

"They are not alone Becky, they have each other!"

Chapter 6 – This Little Piggy

"You're really mean. How would you like to stay out here?"

"Might be a step up if your mother's in a bad mood."

"Yeah, you're funny. But you're still mean."

"Don't get too attached Becky, these babies will wind up on the table in a few months."

"I know, but I get to take care of them now and they should be in the house!"

"Okay, I'll tell you what. Get your mother's permission and I'll let you keep them in the basement for a few nights."

"You mean it?"

"Absolutely, go talk to her right now."

I continued spreading hay in the little pen. She was gone for about 10 minutes and I was starting to worry that her mother might agree with her. I knew it had worked out when she came back and slammed the door on her way in.

"You knew what she was going to say, didn't you? You are so mean! And she's really swearing a lot lately."

"We'll put up this heat lamp so they get a little warmth out here. In a couple weeks, the frost danger will have passed and we can put them outside."

"I'll help with food and water if you want."

"Yes, I want you to. There's also the job of scooping poop out of their pen."

"Alright, I'll help with that, too," she said, wearing a great big smile from ear to ear.

I told her again not to get terribly attached to animals that were going to be butchered. She yessssed me and I went back into the house. After a couple of hours, I noticed that Becky wasn't in the house. As I was heading back into the garage, I stopped to look through the window. She was sitting there reading 'Charlotte's Web' to the piglets in the light of the heat lamp. There are no words for the simple joy I felt at that moment.

The next morning at breakfast, I was taken by surprise when very casually, Becky asked what we were going to name the pigs. I pointed out that farm animals usually weren't named because they would be going to the slaughterhouse in a few months. Becky blew that off with a wave of her hand. Then she said, "They need names and if you don't want to participate, then I will name them." Her mother sat there quietly smiling. I was starting to get the idea that this was a done deal long before I woke up.

"Okay Becky, tell us their names," I said.

"I figured," she said, "since you are so close to Sister Norberto, Romuald and Teresa that we should name our babies after them. They'll be Norb, Rom and Tess."

"Should make the trip to the slaughterhouse a little easier."

"And you already know how to deal with their poop." Life would be easier with dumb kids.

I did draw the line at dressing them up as nuns for Halloween.

Building the pigpen was another educational experience for Becky. Primarily rounding out her vocabulary of profanity. I was not the most

Chapter 6 – This Little Piggy

adept carpenter in those parts. When I asked John to come over and take a look at it, he could barely suppress a smile. "Fortunately, it is only for pigs," he said. He told me to run the boards all the way to the ground unless I had two or three hours a day to chase the pigs around after they got loose. I did that. They got loose anyway. Luckily, Becky had a knack of getting them back with just a little coffee can with grain in the bottom leading them back into the pen with its sound.

Throughout the summer Becky diligently fed our not so little pigs at least twice a day. She was more than happy to do that as long as daddy was the one shoveling pig poop. There were many times during that summer that my heart was touched just watching her sitting on the fence rails above the pigs telling them stories. We also had to keep a close eye on Eric. He was still a toddler and getting into the pen was one of his highest priorities. Becky said many times that getting in the pen might improve Eric's aroma.

The chicks had gotten to the house three weeks after the pigs. Because of cold weather, they stayed in the basement until the end of May. The first week was a lot of fun watching the kids heard the peeping little furballs around the basement. That was good for about a week. Slowly but surely the house started smelling like a chicken coop. Eric was the last to notice. His mother was the first. I could no longer wait to put the finishing touches on the chicken coop. This included driving fence posts into nearly frozen ground.

Once again Becky's vocabulary expanded. Two full weekends filled with sweating and swearing got a 10'x15' run built for the chicks. The first thing we noticed was that the holes in the chicken wire were too big. The chicks thought it was a great game. Go in the chicken house, out to the run and then scatter with everyone chasing them. Becky thought if we didn't chase them, maybe they would come back for food and water. I prayed she was wrong. But, she did know her animals. Thus began our summer of discovery of just how filthy chickens really are.

Sober And Miserable

Soon, it was September and Wendy and I were drinking coffee and talking about slaughtering chickens. Somehow, Becky heard the discussion from the backyard and came in with a terrified look on her face. She stood straight, looked right at us and said, "You are not killing my girls." And being the master of the obvious, I asked her if she remembered how cold it had been last winter. And she said, "Of course I do, I'm not stupid," clearly getting worked up for a fight. And fight we did for the next two hours on and off. She'd walk out, slam the door and walk back in 10 seconds later with her index finger raised. She finally said she would feed them and collect the eggs, no matter how much snow and cold she had to walk through. I let it go. I foolishly thought she'd quit after there were a couple of feet of snow on the ground. I was wrong again. We had fresh eggs all winter. And Becky didn't get a cold the entire time. Go figure. My life was about as good as it could be while living under the same roof with a chronically unhappy woman. Of course, she was living under the same roof with a chronically unhappy man.

That first summer of raising pigs was a blur. The weather was warm and dry all the way through October. We were all too busy to get in very much trouble. Without warning Halloween came and went, delivering a bitter cold November. I know it was time to take the pigs for a ride over to Hebron on Newfound Lake. The little slaughterhouse there was known for its cleanliness and fair prices. The butcher told me just to call a few hours ahead so he would know we were coming. I dreaded making that call. I had become attached to those damn pigs. I started thinking about ways to keep them. There were none. God, I felt awful. And instead of doing it right away, I put it off for a week. I must've really needed the pain at that moment. I got to sink lower and lower for seven straight days. I was a brilliant planner. This kind of mood also made arguments with the wife considerably more toxic. I felt shitty about everything and there she was bitching and begging to be blamed for the way I felt.

The Sunday before the ride to the lake, I arranged to borrow Janet and John's pig box. This is a long contraption, heavily built of two by

Chapter 6 – This Little Piggy

fours and nearly 10 feet long. The scenery was that you would put this box in the bed of your pickup truck and entice your pigs to get in there for the ride to their slaughter. Simple enough, I thought. Apparently the first task wasn't simple enough for me. I lifted one end of the pig box into the bed of my truck. And yes, I turned down John's assistance. I was certainly man enough to do this job myself. I picked up the other end of the pig box and deftly slid it into the bed of the truck and through the rear window of the truck. I picked little tiny pieces of glass out of that truck for years. Now I got to go home and be congratulated for my handiwork. This was shaping up to be so much fun. I wondered if anybody had ever committed suicide over taking pigs to butcher. Then, I decided I would keep that thought to myself, lest others not see the humor in it.

I wasn't even out of the truck before my charming wife came out and said, "Oh, I like what you've done with the truck. Should help you stay awake on the long drive home from work." It was 4 miles from home to my office. I spent that Sunday splitting wood for our woodstove trying to rediscover my manliness. All I got were splinters and blisters.

Oh, I did sleep well, but alone that night. I was exhausted. For a while I saw the pigs' faces in each block of wood I hit with an ax. That made me even sadder. But some benevolent spirit intervened and allowed me to see the faces of the nuns the pigs were named for. That brightened my day considerably... I became almost cheery. Even with that boost, I couldn't get my head off the fact that my pigs would be executed the very next day. Becky had gone into hiding and there was no one around to tell me everything would be okay.

Monday was a regular workday and I would have to get through it thinking of the ride facing me that night. Newfound Lake was a very pretty 10-mile long natural lake in central New Hampshire. It was very sparsely populated and extremely quiet in the winter. Winter in New Hampshire was the months other than July and August. I loved driving on the narrow two-lane roads surrounding the lake and the hills beyond.

Sober And Miserable

I consciously chose to take the pigs over at night so I wouldn't be able to see anything unpleasant. I would go, put them in the pen, go home, and come back in a week to pick them up wrapped in butcher paper. And life would go on. Except for Norb, Rom and Tess. Did I mention I hadn't been to a meeting in over a week? No, I guess I didn't. I guess I hadn't even given it a thought.

The day turned out to be unusually warm and went by quickly. I had asked Wendy to pull the truck around in the field by the pig pen to simplify my chores. She had done that and more. The ramp was right by the gate to the pigpen and should've made my job simple. It was such a nice day that Wendy and some of the neighbors went out by the pigpen to have a drink. We lived in a very sophisticated neighborhood, after all. They all seemed to be having a grand time. But, my mood was taking a dive. It just rubbed me the wrong way that they were out there having fun and I was going to have to work all evening. I was right about having to work ALL evening. They were all standing there because the pigs weren't cooperating. They wanted no part of the ramp into the pig box. After a couple more hours of trying to coax the pigs into the box, my humor was now completely foul. And my wife and neighbors were half in the bag.

The next brilliant idea involved giving the pigs alcohol. The three of them swelled a pint of alcohol in record time. Then they wanted more. Who knew? They got really pissed and ran into the fence trying to get out over and over again. My shotgun came to mind and I wondered for a moment if the butcher would accept them dead. I dropped that idea but my mind was still hooked on how much vodka those damn pigs had spilled. I knew it must be getting late when I saw Becky walking across the field towards us in her pajamas.

"How come I didn't get invited to the party?" she asked.

"Damn pigs won't get in the box," I said.

Chapter 6 – This Little Piggy

"I told them you're going to kill them."

"Thanks Becky, that explains a lot."

"Still want 'em in the box?"

"Well, yeah!"

I hadn't noticed that she had a plastic bowl in her hands filled with quartered apples. She took a few of them and threw them up in the front of the box and the biggest pig, Norb, plowed into the box like a linebacker. Two more apples and the other pigs were firmly ensconced in their temporary home. It had taken a very little girl almost 15 minutes to do what four adults couldn't accomplish in over two hours. She brushed her hands off and went back in the house. By the time I moved the truck around to the front and had gone to her room, she was asleep. It was nearly 10 o'clock and I thought it would be a good idea if I went to bed and took the pigs over early in the morning.

After all the exercise and excitement, sleep came quickly…and left just as quickly. I parked the pigs in my truck in the driveway at least 50 feet from our bedroom windows. Their snoring was so loud it would still keep me awake after I closed the windows. The pigs were so sloshed that when I went down to shake them they didn't even wake up. I surrendered my night. It was a completely black attitude. I got dressed to take the pigs over to the slaughterhouse. I was exhausted but I wanted to get this miserable job done. As I drove towards the lake in the dark, my mood collapsed. I was angry and wanted to blame someone. My feelings were all over the place. The vodka had looked good, really good. Why did I get sucked into having pigs anyway?

They were nothing but a pain in the ass. And then the deepest emotional pit I had, opened up. Why didn't this woman love me? She was such an inconsiderate bitch. I'd had it. I put up with her for more than

Sober And Miserable

10 years and there was still no peace. I was done. A human whale wallowing on the bottom of the emotional ocean.

The town of Hebron came into view. First thing I saw were the pens at the slaughterhouse. When I got there, I backed the truck around to an open pen. I got out, open the gate, dropped the pig box and shooed the pigs out. I felt nothing. Right then, I hated everyone. Including me. Everything was wrong. As I got to the south end of the lake I remembered there was a little bar just before Ragged Mountain Road. It just made sense. I needed a drink. It was what had been missing.

The strange thought that I needed a drink and could get one in a few minutes relaxed both my body and mind. I didn't think for a moment about sobriety. The need was intense and immediate. I had been in the desert and there was finally some water. There is no problem with justification. I was pretty well self-justified on a daily basis due to the fools and idiots I had to tolerate.

The bar was a low, one-story affair with bright neon beer signs in the front windows. There were only a couple of pickup trucks in the parking lot but it was almost midnight. I sat there for a second before he opened the door of the truck. What would I order? It had been so long. In less than a second, the thought of a shot and a beer was in my head and my mouth was salivating. I walked over to the door and grabbed a shaky old doorknob. It turned but the door wouldn't open. I tried again and when it still wouldn't open, I kicked the bottom. I walked around the side, and through an open window, saw that it was dark and no one was there. Well, that was weird. I knew I would have taken a drink if that place had been open. There was another bar 15 miles closer to home but I just as quickly had no interest. What a night.

I knew I had come close to drinking. For some reason, probably alcoholism, I didn't react as if I had just walked away from a near fatal collision. The best I could come up with was that I was overtired. A seriously

Chapter 6 – This Little Piggy

lame excuse for almost pulling the trigger on this Russian roulette game I could only lose. By not going to meetings, not talking with anybody about how I felt, letting all the stress in my life control me, I had cut my lifelines. My life immediately drifted into deep water and I hadn't even noticed. I felt good walking up to the front door of that bar. In an instant, I had lost my sanity. It stuns me now to realize I had no consciousness of what I was doing. My intention was to drink and I was perfectly okay with that idea. But I didn't drink. That puzzled me. But, not excessively so. A lucky coincidence? I still couldn't acknowledge the power of God.

Chapter 7

Ballistic Sobriety

Wikipedia loosely defines ballistics as the science of mechanics that deals with the flight, behavior and effects of projectiles. They go on to say that these projectiles are only "guided" during the relatively brief initial powered phase of flight. They identify three phases of ballistic flight: 1.Powered flight 2.Free flight and 3.Re-entry/impact. I am well aware that the foregoing description is intended to be applied to missiles and bombs and rockets and such. It also provides a very close replica of too many self-managed programs of recovery. There's also a concept known as "escape velocity". This is where the projectile leaves the bonds of Earth's gravity and circles the planet with no additional fuel needed. This speed is approximately 8 mi./s. This concept is not applicable to addiction and alcoholism. Many have thought that a good and sound initial fueling of the right literature and right associates would allow them to orbit sobriety from afar.

I met my friend Todd at a fundraiser for the Hope House. It was our local halfway house for alcoholics in Bangor, Maine. It was in a 1940s vintage Air Force barracks on what was the old Dow Air Force Base. It was now adjacent to the newly christened Bangor International Airport. The building was old and ugly but clean and quite serviceable. There was a friendly and warm place for twenty men who would not survive the winter on the street in Bangor. There was a counselor available, a part-time nurse, a volunteer doctor and daily visitors from local recovery groups. Money still needed to be raised for incidentals like fuel oil

Chapter 7 – Ballistic Sobriety

that was needed for heat 10 months of the year. I knew the doctor that volunteered, and he had invited me to this fundraiser. Todd was a big, good-looking guy who was marketing director for a huge media outlet. I naturally gravitated toward him because all the women were standing around him. This would become a common theme with Todd. It must be instinctual in men to go where the women are.

Anyway, I introduced myself to Todd and he started introducing me to the women that had surrounded him. Several were board members of Hope House. They cornered me and moved me away from the group and I realized I had been set up. Before I left that day, I was the newest member of their board.

As I was getting in my car, Todd yelled to me and asked if I wanted to get a drink. I told him I'd be happy to go with them but that I didn't drink. He walked over and when he was about 3 feet from me, he asked if I was a friend of Bill. I told him I was and he smiled at me said he was, too. We both laughed a little and decided to go to a little coffee shop downtown. It was so comfortable that it seemed like it was something we had done every day for a long time. At the time, I was sober about eight years and he, four. That first afternoon, we talked about our lives. He had a typically unhappy upbringing and was happy to be living in Maine, far from his family of origin. My own life was in a bit of a shambles at the moment. My wife and I had separated when she was living in Michigan with her mother, with little interest in returning to me or Maine. We were perfect co-commiserators. His biggest fear in life was being without a woman. Mine was being with a woman, the wrong one. This was apparently fertile ground for friendship.

After a brutal Maine winter, May rolled around with blinding blue skies and lupines blooming everywhere…the purple flowers letting us know that nature had exhaled and winter had finally gone to bed. Todd called me one morning and asked if we could meet for lunch in Camden. This little harbor and village surrounding it may be the most charming spot on a coast with hundreds of beautiful places.

Sober And Miserable

But, it was an hour from town and I wondered what was going on. I knew he was having a problem and that was enough reason for me to head over there and we set a time for late lunch. I hadn't been in Camden during the winter and was suddenly very excited about sitting beside its really cold Harbor and looking at the old schooners with winter covers still in place.

Todd had gotten there before me and had a table on the harbor facing Mount Battie, the huge granite mound that rose directly behind the town. I was grateful the restaurant had left the plastic windscreens in place. Even with a blazing sun, the temperature was still in the 50s and it would've been damned uncomfortable if the dining area was open to the elements. But, the outside dining was perfect that day. Immediately in front of us, was the fleet of tall ships that kept tourists busy all summer. You could go out for a day or a week. There were also a couple of small sailboats rushing the season just a bit in their eagerness to begin the summer. Off to the left, the view was of the waterfall that ran off the mountain at the head of the harbor. I could sit there for hours with the sites and the intoxicating smell of the ocean. The added bonus of being chilly, was the absence of crowds and near silence except for the occasional swearing worker on the water.

Todd stood up to shake my hand and gave me a half hug at the same time.

"So, my friend, what's the cause of the special occasion?" I asked.

"Yeah, sort of feels like a date doesn't it?" Todd said, smiling.

"It better not be! I thought you liked women."

"Ah, you are an asshole aren't you?"

"You did call me."

Chapter 7 – Ballistic Sobriety

"Next time, I'll tell your secretary that it's not a homo call."

"Okay, I guess. No camping trips, though. Now, what the hell did you want?"

"I would like it very much if you would be my sponsor."

"Sure. We could have done this on the phone, you know."

"I guess we could have…if neither one of us had any class."

We laughed a little and talked for the next two hours. Mostly about a woman he had met in town, that he thought was going to change his life. He thought he was in love. I thought it was scary. I wish I had known this little fact before agreeing to sponsor him. I was pretty sure I could help him with his recovery program. I had been around long enough to know that alcoholics are uniquely unqualified to consult on romantic relationships. It would be a very rough ride.

The formal part of my sponsorship with Todd went well. We went through the big book of Alcoholics Anonymous by reading two chapters each week. He wasn't new to the program but I was impressed with his enthusiasm for the book and the lessons that it held. He quickly understood that each step related to the next one in order and that any neglect of details would be carried forward to undermine his effort in the following steps. We had long discussions about his character defects and how he might work on them to help him "clean house" as was mentioned in the big book. There was the predictable difficulty with trying to understand how spirituality comes into a recovering alcoholics life. I was having the same trouble at the same time. My spiritual life didn't develop until I realized that, for me, it was not an intellectual process.

Spirituality only manifested in my life when I accepted the notion that I was on this planet to provide loving service to my fellow man. This idea can be talked about forever. I gained nothing and didn't change a bit until I got off my ass and reached out to men in prison. There are many other things I've done to get out of my comfort zone and be available for others. I had to get over discomfort, before I could grow spiritually.

For the first couple of months, Todd was a great sponsee. We met regularly, went to several meetings per week together, and broke bread at least once a week. It seemed we both grew exponentially during this period. Then, one week in early fall, Todd dropped completely off the radar. I left messages for him at work and at home. I was really kind of concerned. He had a little trailer he kept way out in the woods and I even went out and checked that. No Todd. The following Monday, I stopped by his office early in the morning and caught him as he was coming in to work.

"Excuse me sir, do you recognize me?" I asked.

"Oh hi, how have you been?" he replied.

"Did you lose my number?"

"What's the matter?"

"Are you kidding me? You blew off our meetings, you didn't show for lunch or even call. And you ask me what's the matter?"

"Oh man, this relationship thing has really taken off. It's beyond my wildest dreams. She is the one I've been looking for."

"Have you been drinking?"

"No, I mean it. This is the real deal. Aside from work, I spent every waking and sleeping moment with her!"

Chapter 7 – Ballistic Sobriety

"Jesus Christ! Are you telling me you've moved in with her?"

"Really, it's okay. I've been sleeping there every night but I haven't moved in."

"Did it ever occur to you that you might want to run this by your sponsor?"

"Man, this took me out like a wave on the beach that I never saw coming. All of a sudden, I'm waking up in the morning in her bed feeling like I've been there for years. I've always dreamed of something like this and didn't think it could happen for me."

"Have you set a date yet?"

"No. Well, we did talk about it one night, but that was just dreamy talk."

"You are off the reservation, kimosabe. This little fling of yours has already taken you miles off the path of recovery and you don't even know it."

"You're overreacting! I fell in love and took a little vacation…that's all. I haven't quit recovery. I still feel good, actually better than ever, and don't want to drink or drug."

"Hang onto that thought, Buster! You need to remember how you got to the point of not wanting to drink or drug. From what I hear, that goes away a lot easier than it comes."

"Really, I'll give you a call and we can go to a meeting Wednesday night, okay?"

"Okay. Don't forget!"

Sober And Miserable

In case you were wondering, no, he didn't call and he didn't show up Wednesday night. It was Sunday night at the meeting in Orono before I ran into him again. His face immediately turned red as he stammered out an apology. He launched into a monologue about how blessed his life was and how grateful he felt to have such a wonderful woman in his life. In two weeks, he had gone from a person dedicated to his sobriety, to a man on the outskirts of recovery intoxicated with the flush of a new relationship. He actually had the nerve to tell me that his gratitude for this woman could keep him sober. I knew he hadn't been drinking but he almost sounded as if he had. I stood there watching him as if he were a boat drifting out to sea from his moorings. Above everything else, I felt helpless. After the meeting was over, he went straight to his car and went on without even saying goodnight.

After that night, I rarely saw Todd. I called him a few times but he never returned calls. Over the next year, I saw him at meetings two or three times. He always made a point of coming over to me, giving me a big handshake and a smile and telling me how wonderful his life was. He was now blissfully ensconced in this lady's house. In that year following my attempt to be a sponsor for Todd, I actually had an opportunity to meet and get to know his girlfriend. She was the director of a local charity and an outstanding fundraiser. She was a very pretty, high-energy woman who gave the impression that she was going places. I wondered how much she would enjoy Todd's ramshackle trailer in the woods. Maybe I was a little bit jealous.

Over the course of that year, my life changed quite a bit, as well. My wife decided to come back to Maine and for her trouble, I got her pregnant. Six or eight weeks before our son's birth, Todd showed up unexpectedly at our front door. It was a brutally cold early January night. He looked like he had been drinking. That wasn't the case, even though he was as miserable as if he had been. I brought him right in the house, took his coat and walked him into the warm kitchen.

Chapter 7 – Ballistic Sobriety

"Are you okay?" I asked.

"No," he said weakly.

"So my friend, spill it!"

"She threw me out."

"What did you do?"

"Nothing. It came out of the blue. It was fine one night and the next morning at the breakfast table, she quietly told me I was gonna have to leave."

"No explanation?"

"She said she was just done, that she had never expected it to last forever. She said she enjoyed every minute of it. She'll probably send me a thank you note. I'm lost. I don't know what to do."

"Well, you can start to return to normalcy by loading up on meetings. You and I can go back to having lunch once a week. Maybe even discussing some interesting shit."

"Yeah, I'll think about that. What can I do about her? She's all I think about. I don't know if I can live without her."

"You seemed to do okay before she came along."

"Not really. I was adrift before I met her."

"I disagree! You had purpose and a path that you had chosen to follow."

Sober And Miserable

"I don't know. I feel lost."

We sat down and chatted for a couple of hours. I tried to remind him of the Fellowship of recovery in the good times we had before his girlfriend came along. I tried to let him know that his horrible feelings of loss and loneliness would pass in time. He was devastated because he had been so serious while she really looked at it as just an extended fling. The reason for his visit was simply for me to give him ideas about getting her back. I wasn't very motivated to do that, largely because it seemed obvious to me that she, in fact, was done. Less than a month later, she would move to Boston. And he would know new pain. He was truly in a free-fall at this point. Her move to Boston was, in his mind, done solely as a final insult to him and their relationship.

Over the next six weeks, I saw him in no more than two or three meetings. He was always bleak, huddled in a corner or in the back row. We always smiled and said hello to each other but that was where it ended. On March 1st that year, my son Eric was born at home in a driving Maine snowstorm. Once again, my life changed dramatically. For the better. I entered a new period of happiness and felt close to the good things in life. My little son was a treasure to me. I was well aware he was a wonderful product, of a not so wonderful, relationship.

Early one evening while his mother was out shopping, I sat in a rocking chair, rocking that little boy to sleep with great pleasure. The phone was on the table next to me and it rang at exactly 6 o'clock. Michael, one of my other sponsors, was on the phone saying that he hated to have to give me bad news. He told me that Todd had gone home from the meeting the night before and ran a hose from his car into the trailer. He had been found this morning by one of the deputies on patrol. He told me Todd had died peacefully. I knew differently. I sat and rocked Eric until I stopped crying. That little life in my arms anchored me to something much greater that my distorted, alcoholic thoughts. I felt grateful for maybe the first time in my life.

Chapter 7 – Ballistic Sobriety

Yes, I called my sponsor that night. I briefly told him what had happened and we agreed to have a therapeutic lunch the next day. I felt more than a little urgency but thought it was just about Todd. Wrong, as usual, when it came to understanding my own feelings. For me, urgency always preceded flight. I wanted to suggest to my sponsor that we meet in Camden but he was a crusty old fisherman and thought Camden was prissy…at best! He chose the dirtiest little diner Bangor had to offer. He was oblivious to the dirt and grease and was always comfortable there. He even thought the food was good. I didn't pick him as a sponsor for his culinary acumen. He was sober thirty years and had what seemed like a hundred years of insight. He was pulling into the parking lot as I got out of my car.

"Hi John, it's really good to see you," I said.

"Guess you must've had a tough night, huh?" John said, as we walked towards the diner and he put his arm around my shoulders.

"Yeah, I didn't get much sleep."

"There's going to be a fair amount of nights like that if you insist on working with drunks."

"Jesus, I guess you've seen a few."

"We do wind up burying quite a few of them. It's a wicked disease."

"It's got me really turned around, John."

"I know, I came here for you. There's nothing we can do for Todd except maybe learn from his shortcomings."

"Isn't that a bit harsh?"

Sober And Miserable

"Wait till you hear what I say about you! That is, if you can take it in your weakened state."

"Have you been studying on how to be an asshole again?"

"I have. Helps me feel closer to my sponsees."

"So you came here just to beat on me?"

"You didn't think I came here for the food, did you?"

We got the last booth in the furthest corner of the place and ordered our lunch. He didn't even have the courtesy to let me eat before he started in.

"His choices made him dead. He got a break. If you keep making bad choices, you may not be so lucky."

"What the hell do you mean I thought I was doing fine?"

"That's another problem. You 'thought' you're doing fine. Did you validate that self-serving thought with anyone else?"

"Not exactly."

"And that's not even the biggest problem that I see with you."

"Okay, let me have it."

"You suck at problem identification which leads you to solving things that are not actually problems. So, instead of addressing your real problems, you make up new ones that you think you can solve."

"Can you give me any examples?"

Chapter 7 – Ballistic Sobriety

"Oh, in abundance."

"You're enjoying this way too much."

"I do. But on the practical side, you may learn something if you pay attention. Or you may take the route your friend Todd chose and think you know it all. And it's the next lesson that may be the one that saves your ass."

"What about these problems you think I make up?"

"Well, remember that relationship problem you have? The one known as a marriage? Instead of trying to figure out what was wrong with you when she left, you bought a new truck. You did that real well. When you were done with that, the success of your marriage was still hanging in the balance. Your job was giving you nightmares last year. You were absolutely sure the problem was with the board. You invested nothing in trying to discover what you contributed to that situation. Another defective relationship triumph. Right in the middle of all of that, you decide you need to build a brand-new garage at your house. It is a very pretty garage. Your job still hangs in the balance and you don't have a clue about what you are doing wrong. You seem to be completely resistant to handling the job right in front of you. You have to learn to confront fear. At the moment, it is running your life. At the moment, it is your higher power. It almost looks like you've made a decision to turn your will in your life over to your character defects."

"Damn."

"I don't expect you to do anything right this minute. Take a day or two. Think about your dead friend. Ask yourself what happens to a recovering alcoholic when he stops changing. Can you recognize how destructive your ego is and take steps to correct that? Nothing much at stake, just your life."

Then the bastard made me buy lunch.

Chapter 8

Teach Your Parents Well

Sometimes the shift from drunkenness to sobriety is so dramatic that the issue of quality in sobriety is totally unnoticed. In my case, it remained that way for many years. At 15 years sober, I managed to pull off a disappearing trick. I left my unconscious body with my family and my mind departed at warp speed to anywhere else. Having 15 years of sobriety, the thought is: "I must be OK, I've got 15 years." This is very clearly the voice of the disease speaking from a serious blind spot. It allowed my mind to think that I'm only sick when I'm drinking…thereby putting up a smokescreen to hide my character defects from myself. Unfortunately, this is a situation I am much too willing to accept without question. The accouterments of sobriety (money, property and prestige) finish the job of lowering the sheet over my eyes. I have every external thing I've ever wanted. But, is there any other evidence of success? Inside, I felt connected to nothing. I had worked on this canvas of my life for 15 years and when I stepped away from the easel, I couldn't recognize a single thing.

One of the biggest regrets of my life has been missing the connection with my daughter, Becky. I was there but I wasn't. I knew there was so much that was special about her that I should make an effort to be close. My self-absorption allowed little time for anything but me. I put little effort into an emotional connection and virtually none on a spiritual connection. I was drawn to her calm, peaceful spirit. She had an uncanny sense of the moment and an ability to leave people smiling

Chapter 8 – Teach Your Parents Well

when she left the room. Instead of drawing close to this child and spending time with her, I spent my time enmeshed in the muck of my life created by my unaddressed character defects. There was little room for anyone else in my life. Even without alcohol, my life was still a dark battle. Although Becky was as radiant as the sun, I was so blinded by my self-seeking that I couldn't realize that it was her light that I craved. I told myself I had accepted life as a struggle, put on my big boy pants and went after the win. To this day, I am in awe of the resilience of these little human beings.

In the end, Becky was the saving grace of these very troubled years in my life. From the time she was six until she was 16 we lived in New Hampshire and Pennsylvania. The setting was beautiful, safe and very supportive for children. The area was full of decent, concerned, generally loving people. We wound up there because I had accepted a job running the local hospital in Lebanon, New Hampshire. Not ideal but a good job anyway.

My ability to appreciate what I had still had not matured. The marriage was not working. Becky's mother was sour and her father was angry. Two months before moving to New Hampshire, we had just had our son, Eric. From the outside, it looked like a storybook family. The inside was a very different story…it could've been written by Mary Shelley. Our relationship was barely civil at this time. We went through long, cold silences, all punctuated with verbally violent outbursts. I told myself I was staying because no decent man would leave two little children. In my own mind, "she" was at fault. I had become a self-justified martyr. If I left, I would be seen as the villain. Of course, then I would have to deal with all my negative feelings that I had become habituated at blaming on her. I had become comfortable with blaming her. It took a sponsor with courage to confront me and point out that the blaming was a manifestation of my own self-pity and that I had better wake up or I would get drunk. I wallowed in my rejection. During this time, I was pretty much unreachable. This particular quality is quite effective if you want to spend most of your time alone. I am so grateful that my children didn't take this opportunity to run away. I bet they wanted to, though!

Becky's mother was a very pretty woman. I'd noticed that almost immediately when we met. I saw a soft loving smile, bright blue eyes and a slender, attractive body. For nearly 15 years, my brain (the one that didn't have a high regard for facts) tried to convince me that there had to be something beautiful inside, as well. But, no, even after I had been exposed to years of that churning cauldron of meanness that lay just below the surface, I still expected there to be something else nice to exist. If I could have accepted her exactly as she was, we both would've been far better off…and divorced 10 years sooner.

Instead, we played yo-yo with our lives for 10+ years. We moved to Pennsylvania and a couple of months later she moved back to New Hampshire and filed for divorce. In a year, she moved back to Pennsylvania to be with me. Six months later she was out again. God must love irony. It was years before I would realize that all this moving back and forth, separating, getting together with more self-indulgent drama was a childish dance put on by two people who in practice didn't give two shits about their children. We acted as if nothing was happening to them. In fact, we both had the audacity to expect them to provide comfort and support for us.

By this time, I knew a divorce was coming. In spite of all my dreams of her running off an icy road to her death, nothing was ever that simple. Apparently, I wasn't meant to be the sad, grieving widower. As luck would have it, she managed to fall in love with her therapist. One weekend when she was supposed to be out of town and visiting friends in New Hampshire, she passed me in traffic. She went right to the house of her therapist. When she returned home on Sunday, I asked her how New Hampshire was and she said that it had been fine. I told her I had followed her the day before and that I wanted her out of the house.

Chapter 8 – Teach Your Parents Well

While the discussion was acrimonious, there was no yelling and screaming. She tried confrontation saying that I couldn't put her out of the house and she was only over talking with her friend, the therapist. Something in me wanted to believe this. This is just further proof that I was an idiot. I found my testicles and told her that if she didn't return by 5PM with a rental agreement, I would take all of her stuff and her personal possessions, put them on the front lawn and set fire to them. It was a little disappointing when she actually returned with a rental agreement. Two months after our divorce was final, they were married. In my heart, I had always known she would find someone else. But why such an asshole? What a humiliation! God must still smile when he thinks of this situation. Unlubricated humility. Guess that's the only kind I actually remember.

I put on a brave face but I was a mess. My victimization at the hands of this woman was complete. Self-pity was on display for the whole world to see. I was pathetic. With no prompting at all, my children and particularly Becky, launched a rescue mission. Fortunately, I was blessed with a lot of time with them. Their mother was in love with the asshole and didn't have much time for them. Both of them attended to me. They hugged and cuddled with me when we watched television. In the morning, as I made breakfast, Becky asked me almost every day

"How's the old man doing today? You gonna kick some butt today?"

She was 14 and Eric was nine. When she got home in the afternoon, she managed to call me in the office to tell me that there had been a vote and we were having pizza for dinner. As I came out of my funk, I was more than a little embarrassed that my children had been so moved to help me. In reality, I was probably incapable of being a decent father at that point. In many subtle ways, Becky made it very clear that she wasn't angry with me over the divorce. She did tell me though that I would be in grave physical danger if I had any thoughts about getting back together with her mother. I took her at her word.

I cringe when I think about how much the divorce must have hurt my children. Neither of us was there for them. My alcoholism was raging and manifesting itself as extreme self-centered behavior. I didn't drink and I did go to meetings. I tried to make my irresponsible life look like it was responsible. I was moody and cranky. Also, frequently angry. My children were living with the Hulk. The fact that so much goodness came out of them at this time is miraculous. Fortunately for me, Becky was brutally honest. If she thought I was being a jerk, she would tell me just that. I also caught her on a number of occasions telling neighbors and family friends about how well I was doing.

During the winter, I had been on a business trip and expected to come home to a cold, empty house. While I had been away, we had gotten about 6 inches of snow. I was very surprised to find that someone had shoveled my driveway. When I walked in the house, I got the great gift of Becky sitting at the kitchen table smiling over a bowl of soup. She had gotten her mother to bring her to my house so that she could shovel the driveway. When she told me this I couldn't stop the tears from rolling down my face. Smiling, she said, "Oh dad, you're such a puss!"

She was also especially able to channel her love to animals. She lied about her age to work as a volunteer at the local animal shelter. She got into horse camp even after the owner told her she was too young. Being able to convince the owner that she knew enough about horses wouldn't be a problem. On the ride out to this camp in Dublin, New Hampshire, she was so excited she practically buzzed. The farm was breathtakingly beautiful. It seemed like miles of white board fence, perfect green grass and great orange daylilies everywhere. The red barn and bunkhouse had been freshly painted. The owner's home was a very traditional New England Cape surrounded with sugar maples. As we were driving in the lane, Becky got very serious, almost solemn. "I'm going to this camp. She'll let me in. I am old for my age, you know," she said.

Chapter 8 – Teach Your Parents Well

All I could think about was having to bring her home after such a big rejection. She had no fear. I had enough for everyone. As Becky walked away with the director of the camp, she was chattering away before they even got in the house. I spent the next hour terrified. I desperately wanted her to get in, but in the pit my stomach I knew she was going to be disappointed. When she came out of the house with the director her face was lit up like a jack-o'-lantern. I could've done backflips right there. When I sat down with the director, I was happy that she didn't know I would have paid 10 times as much money just for the look on her face. She spent her two weeks that year, and many years after, full of joy just to be with her horses. Horse poop and dust became the main ingredients of her favorite perfume.

After 15 years in recovery, I was still so self-absorbed that I couldn't pull myself away from my quest for comfort and self-satisfaction, in order to connect with this gift of a child. Even while still married to her mother, I had little actual time to spend with her. In my twisted little mind, I thought, "Well, you provide the money and the goodies," and I believed that bought absolution for being an absent father. I bragged about all the time I had spent in cold horse barns, watching Becky ride around in circles. Oh, did I mention that I paid for all of those lessons? I was quite a guy!

During a rare moment of consciousness, I had the opportunity to watch her work with her horse, Ruben James. I sat on the back steps of our house while she and Rubin were in the paddock about 50 yards away. The barn and the paddock were very rustic, made of rough local lumber. I had enjoyed building the barn and Becky helped as much as she could. As she walked out of the stall, she rubbed his mane and practically cooed in his ear, "Oh, Boo you are so beautiful! We're gonna have a nice ride today, aren't we?"

She groomed him with brushes bigger than her hands, talking to him all the while. She patted his big chestnut rump, never losing physical contact with him and she deftly, and one-handedly heaved his blanket off the fence and smoothed it onto his back. She never stopped her constant patter with him. His eyes never left her. She even managed to take her saddle off the fence, put it on her shoulder and with one hand, guide it to his back. By the time she was finished cinching his saddle in place, she was pretty much drenched in sweat. Becky and Boo were totally focused on the moment and alive as any two creatures could possibly hope to be. The picture of Becky in the saddle, leaning over to hug Boo's neck before they rode off, is the one I keep in my head to remind me that spirituality really does exist.

Through our years in New Hampshire and Pennsylvania, I suffered with rheumatoid arthritis and it's attendant pain. Even more difficult to cope with than the pain, was the way RA would completely exhaust my energy and motivation. When I was most affected, I had no energy to do even the simplest of things. My wife, subtle thing that she was, insisted that I was merely lazy and unmotivated. I already felt guilty about having so little energy and her constant criticism did nothing but fuel my anger. The love I had for her was eroded on a daily basis. When we had to be together, the atmosphere was arctic. Becky and Eric were the innocent victims as we played our game of dueling character defects. We were both too stubborn to quit, lest the other claim victory.

I went to meetings almost every night. On most nights, I tried to take one or both of the children with me. Eric would only go if I could promise there would be cookies at the meeting or pizza afterwards. He grew up to be a chef. What a surprise! Becky, however, went with me whenever I asked her to go. She was friendly and sweet with everyone she met. If a young woman was sharing her story, Becky would hang on her every word. We had some interesting conversations on the ride home.

One beautiful fall evening, I chose to go to the meeting held in Lyme, New Hampshire. We had our meeting in the town library at

Chapter 8 – Teach Your Parents Well

8PM, after it had closed for the day. It was one of those crisp nights, the trees all Technicolor, with most of the people for the meeting standing around outside talking about how beautiful the night was. As Becky walked into the library, she noticed two older women she had met the week before. She ditched me immediately and went over to them. They were all smiles and happy to see each other and Becky chattered away about the riding lesson she had that day at Morton Farm. She had a wonderful intensity about horses that she shared with those two ladies. She bubbled and she told them of her plans to have a horse farm when she grew up.

The older woman, a very wise and soft spoken 70-year-old who had lived her whole life in New Hampshire said, "Becky, you won't have to wait very long, you truly love horses. And, girl, you are already an old soul." Becky just stood there staring at her. About then, the meeting was starting and she pulled up a little kindergarten chair and sat right next to me. She usually found something to read or eat, but this night she seemed suddenly to have withdrawn. She was still silent after the meeting and when she got in the car, I asked her if something was wrong. She turned her whole body 90° and glared at me.

"You can keep your friend Mary, I don't like her!" she said.

"I thought you two were becoming friends," I said.

"Yeah, and we were until she called me an old hole."

"Oh Becky, she said you were an old soul. That's really a compliment, you know!"

"Well, she'd better keep her compliments to herself," she sniffed.

That night, after the kids were in bed, I shared this with her mother. It was the first time in many years she and I had laughed together.

Sober And Miserable

Later that year, after I had accepted a job in the Boston area, we moved to the quaint colonial town of Amherst, NH. We found a beautiful little house about a mile from the village that dated back to the revolutionary war. There was a village green, surrounded by grand old churches with tall steeples and beautiful old homes built in the early 1700s. The grade school that Becky would go to was a couple of hundred yards off the green. The whole village was a picture of traditional peace and tranquility. Our home was comfortable and simple with the charms of many New England Capes. The house was guarded by huge, old pine trees while the front and side of the house was home to the most beautiful sugar maples I had ever seen. The end of the road we lived on had a beautiful little natural lake that had lifeguards in the summer and ice skating in the winter. The house was perfect! The entire town was almost idyllic. This would finally make us happy.

Wrong again. The so-called adults that lived in that house were, neither very adult, or very happy. She was perpetually disappointed and I was always angry because she was perpetually disappointed. At least, that was why I thought I was angry. She thought she was disappointed because I was disappointing. I would salve my anger with bigger dreams, boring jobs and higher credit limits. Her pretty face turned down at all the worst places with her petulance. If nothing about the marriage is good, at least it provides a handy person to blame. My solution to the cornucopia of relationship problems was to buy 12 acres and build a new house. I would build my dream house!

The morning of January 28, 1986 was very cold in spite of the dazzling sunshine. I had planned to take the family out to the building site and let them see how beautiful it was. On the way over to the lot, we heard on the radio that space shuttle Challenger had exploded 73 seconds into its flight, killing all aboard. I was numb as we walked the property. Between the news and the cold, we were all ready for home after only 30 minutes. After the kids were in the car, Wendy asked me if I thought that Becky would be OK. I said I thought we should ask her

Chapter 8 – Teach Your Parents Well

when we got home. By the time we got home, it was time to start lunch. As I walked in the kitchen to help, Wendy grabbed my arm and said "We should talk to Becky before she gets depressed."

"What?" I said, incredulously.

"Well, Krista McAuliffe was the teacher that lived just 20 miles away."

"Concord is more like 50 miles."

"You know what I mean!"

"No, I really don't."

We marched into the family room where Becky has already turned on the TV and made a cocoon for herself out of an old Afghan blanket. Just her face stuck out of her little nest. She didn't even look at us as we came in the room. We took separate chairs facing her. She noticed us and turned the sound down on the TV.

"OK, what did I do?" she said with an absolutely straight face.

"No, it's nothing like that, sweetheart," I said.

"We were just wondering if you were OK."

"Well," she said, "I'm still a little cold but I'll be OK, I think."

"No," her mother said, "Are you upset about the shuttle?"

"Noooo," she said. "It sucked but I'm fine."

We sat there for a minute until she turned her eyes away from us and brought the sound back up on the TV. We walked back into the kitchen and had to accept that she was truly alright. Wendy seemed disappointed. About three hours later, the phone rang and, of course, it was for Becky. Ten or 15 minutes later, she came into the living room and asked, "Do you know what NASA stands for now?"

We were both baffled and just shook our heads.

"Need Another Seven Astronauts." She smiled, and said, "Like it?"

"You're terrible!" Wendy exclaimed.

"Less than seven hours might be a new record for a disaster joke," I said.

Humor always trumps drama. Becky has taught me so much about life. Her spirit is divine and sublime at the same time. Her God may be sarcasm. Or, more likely, humor. She has always had a sense of what was important and very little patience for the trivial, pretentious and arrogant.

One of her finest moments came four months before Eric was born. We were living in Orrington, Maine, a tiny village on the Penobscot River, about 8 miles east of Bangor. It had been a breathtakingly beautiful fall day. It had been warm for late October, especially in Maine. Becky had played outside all afternoon. I had gotten home from work a little bit early and found Becky sitting at the dining room table, staring out at the beautiful afternoon. I asked her what she was looking at, and she said very softly, "My trees."

"Which ones are your favorites?"

"The orange ones, today."

"They are maple trees, you know."

Chapter 8 — Teach Your Parents Well

"I know that!"

Four years old with an unspoiled confidence.

The table had been set with placemats, silverware and dinner plates. Her mother had just poured Becky's milk and was moving away with the pitcher when she stopped and turned toward Becky. She hesitated for a moment and said with a smirk, "Hey, Beck, if Mommy and Daddy get divorced, who would you want to live with?" Becky continued staring straight-ahead, never looking at her mother and said very evenly, "The Lloyds." They were our neighbors. I bet God was rolling around on the floor!

Chapter 9

Surrender

I had been in Miami for six weeks and the world was looking pretty sweet. The job was falling into place very nicely and I actually thought I might enjoy it. Good things seemed to be happening. There was even a girl who was trying to get me to go to her favorite Cuban restaurant. This was Georgia Brown, a very high energy, fundraiser who always had a pretty smile for everyone. She promised me that this was the most unpretentious and best Cuban food in Miami. When I told her I had never had Cuban food, she was all the more insistent. I knew the time would come when I wouldn't be able to resist her invitations any longer. And so it was on this warm late October night, that I was finally cornered and I agreed that I would catch an early dinner with her.

I was a little surprised at the excitement I felt simply having dinner with a friendly person. Ok, a very attractive, friendly person. She gave me directions to the restaurant, which was on Coral Way and only about five minutes from the office.

The Banyan and strangler figs covered the road with a canopy of green that stretched from curb to curb. As I got out of my car, I was almost knocked over by the intoxicating scent of jasmine. That particular smell will always remind me of the good parts of Miami. Of course, the parts are few enough that it is easy to keep track. In the next mile or two of coral way, it seemed like every third shop front was a restaurant. And the one we were meeting at was among the most modest. It was all

Chapter 9 – Surrender

bright fluorescent lights, plastic tables and paper napkins. And at six o'clock, it was empty. That caused me a bit of concern. Was I going to be stood up? When I realized what I was thinking, I was actually a bit embarrassed. It wouldn't have been the first time I was ever stood up. I decided to wait in front of the restaurant and enjoy the soft scent of jasmine and the saltwater just a block away.

My shoulders dropped from up around my ears and relaxed, and I was suddenly very comfortable as I saw Georgia coming down the street. She was dressed in the same outfit from work with the addition of a big friendly smile. I was so relieved to see her, I was almost giddy.

We went into the restaurant and the ancient waitress told us to sit wherever we would like. We laughed and took a seat by the window and I pulled out her white plastic chair, as a gentleman would. They brought us a basket of Cuban bread and coffee. I asked Georgia what was good at this restaurant and she replied that anything that had pork in it was excellent. It had been a very long time since I had sat with a woman over a meal looking forward to conversation.

I felt I had been in pursuit of life for so many years that I had never really enjoyed it. Now, it felt like things were finally coming together for me. I had been 28 years without a drink and stayed continuously active in recovery. I felt good about all of that. For the first time, maybe in my life, I felt comfortable in my own skin. Not so much entitled, as accepting of my life exactly as it unfolded.

Georgia and I sat side by side, teasing each other about how much bread we were eating, when that annoying little cell phone started chirping. I had every intention of ignoring it until I noticed the caller ID indicated it was from my son's phone in Pennsylvania. Even though I had talked to him a couple of hours ago, it still seemed odd that he would call me again so soon. I answered the call and was immediately startled to hear the voice of his evil stepfather.

Sober And Miserable

"Yes, Bernie," I said.

"I have to tell you that Eric was just taken out of here in an ambulance. It looks like he overdosed. He's unresponsive, paralyzed and not able to breathe on his own," he announced in a voice that sounded like he was reading a menu.

"What the hell happened? I just talked to him an hour ago and he was ok. He didn't even sound like he was upset about anything or that he was using any drugs or alcohol."

"Well, we think it might've been a suicide attempt."

"I just can't believe that!"

"Well, I've got to go," he said and hung up without waiting for me to say anything.

This sudden collision of feelings felt like a physical blow and came close to knocking me out of my chair. It was as if I had been dropped in freezing cold water. I sat there for a minute with the phone in my hand, told Georgia what had happened and that I was going to have to leave. She was very sweet and offered to help in any way she could. She must've paid the bill because it didn't even occur to me. I was dazed as I walked out into the street that had been so welcoming just 10 minutes ago.

I got in the car called USAir but there were no flights from Miami to Philadelphia until the next morning. I went to the place where I was staying, a house used by religious brothers. When I walked in they could all tell there was something wrong. I told them all what happened and they said they would pray for him. I felt disconnected from everything. My outside could have been a robot completely autonomous from the 'me' inside. I was in a place that I had never been before, in my entire life. Poor Georgia was another casualty of the evening. The crisis had

Chapter 9 – Surrender

taken the smile right off her face. It was probably a month before we had any contact and she definitely exuded a chill. She and I would never again exchange anything more intimate than daily pleasantries. My loss.

When I got to my room and closed the door behind me, it felt good to be alone. I got my carry-on bag out and packed for my trip to Pennsylvania. That done, I sat on my bed and realized there was absolutely nothing I could do. My eyes went to the book I had been reading that was sitting on my dresser. It was the 'Tibetan Book of Living and Dying'. For just a second, my feelings went to the place that was linking the book with Eric's situation. I started to feel myself falling and knew I had to drag myself out of this feeling. It was as if I were sitting on the knife edge of a rock with 1000 foot drop on either side. If I look down I would fall. I knew I would be lost to the grief and be unable to function.

Then, I was trapped between two unacceptable realities. It took every bit of emotional energy I had left to resist descending into the fear that lay in the darkness of my thoughts. The only thing that was real was for me to get to Pennsylvania. Nothing else mattered in the slightest. I talked with my God and didn't wonder for a moment if He was listening. I knew He was there. I also knew that this didn't mean that Eric would survive. I felt great sadness but absolutely no fear. It was horrible that Eric had reached the point that taking his own life was the only option he could see. He was 16.

My issues and problems became microscopic. I wanted to sob. In that moment, everything imploded. I had no awareness of anything in the world but my thoughts and feelings. He was just a kid. I thought about him sitting there on the phone telling me everything was okay…yet an hour later taking pills to kill himself. I couldn't believe the amount of pain he had to feel to do that. I couldn't breathe. The terror of thinking of losing him had closed my throat. Fuck, fuck, fuck. I hated myself for having left him there. I should've taken him.

I was floating in ice cold space. The world was gone. I was in hell. Swept away in a river of fear of what lay in front of me. His little face dressed in a paper sunflower kept coming into my head. Him telling me this Montessori teacher was mean and being right after all tortured my memory. I screamed at the thought of having to bury him. And I couldn't breathe again. He got in trouble in preschool defending little girl with a handicap. I wasn't supposed to be, but all I felt for him was pride for being so little and having so much courage. I thought about the day I took him to sign up for Little League. He didn't want to go and he barricaded himself in the doorway. He finally went and became a hot-shot Little Leaguer. We always laughed when we talked about me trying to pull him through that doorway.

He had a killer smile and knew how to use it before he was 10. Oh, God dammit, why didn't I take him away from his mother and that idiot she lived with? His smile came with a kind and gentle heart. Even when he was three or four and we visited our friends Janet and John, he was thrilled just to put his arms around the little lambs. My head kept running these movies of Eric being beautiful. I had no idea I could cry quite so much.

That night, I actually slept for five or six hours. Before lying on my bed, I had assumed I wouldn't get any sleep at all. I was at the airport by 5AM and felt as alone as I had ever felt as an adult. As much as I didn't like to travel all dressed up, I was wearing my best suit, not knowing if I would have to attend a funeral. While waiting, I received a call from his mother telling me he was in ICU and on a ventilator. She said they wouldn't know for a couple days if he would survive. I was thrilled to hear that he was alive at that moment. My prayer was purely of thanks. I was still in that cocoon of shock that kept everything out except my thoughts and prayers for Eric. I wanted desperately for him to live and was deeply aware of the real possibility that he would not. As long as he was alive, I would keep my energy and spirit upon him.

Chapter 9 – Surrender

When I got to the hospital, it was just before noon. Until six years before, I had been Executive Vice President of that hospital. Everybody in ICU remembered me and was quite kind. When I walked into his room, his mother was picking her coat up, moving for the door and told me without meeting my eyes that she was going home to sleep. There were no explanations and no way for me to get a word in.

When I looked at Eric, the only feeling I had was a crushing desire to cry. He lay on the ICU bed with his hands and feet restrained and a machine breathing for him. He looked very thin and his head was shaved bald. His face was bruised around his cheekbones. Over the next few days, I would find out many things about the way they were living. At that moment, I would have given my entire future to have him alive. Although he had not been an especially easy child to raise, he was a special joy for me.

Behind his bluster and occasional anger, he had a wonderful heart. He would come to the defense of smaller children around him and managed to get in trouble regularly by confronting bullies. I spent that first day in the hospital, sitting by his bedside, telling him about all the special times I had with him. I held his hand and rubbed it as I told him about the days we had camped together and gone fishing in the little stream that ran through New Boston. I described how beautiful Lake Sunapee was on his third Christmas and how we had taken a ride in my old pickup truck just to see the snow falling on the partially frozen lake. Even the ride had been quiet as snow provided padding for the bumpy dirt road around the lake. His car seat had been in the middle of the front seat of the truck and he held onto my arm for the entire ride.

Talking with him like this made the day go by and kept my mind out of thoughts of tomorrow. I told him how, when he was three, he had been the scourge of the neighborhood for a couple weeks with his habit of biting people. This included his sister, neighbors and the dog. His mother wanted to take him to a psychologist. Until, that is, he came up

Sober And Miserable

behind her one day while she was on the telephone and bit her so hard on the butt that he almost drew blood. His mother was furious and told me I could do anything I wanted with him. I grabbed his little hand, put it in my mouth and bit down hard on the knuckles. That was the last day he bit anyone. And lastly, I rubbed his hand telling him about our trip to Bayside, Maine and the tiny cottage we stayed in. Tears ran all over my face as soon as I started thinking about the place. The first night we were there, he came down to my room at about midnight. There was noise coming off the water and it woke him and frightened him badly. We went out on the porch where we could see the 50 or 60 sailboats bobbing in the light breeze. We could also plainly hear the halyards as they slapped against the aluminum masts. He was so relieved and he smiled at me and said, "Dad, can we call it halyard music?" I stopped talking to Eric at that point and just looked at him in that bed, happy to have that moment to hang on to.

Later that evening, his mother returned. She complained bitterly about Eric and how difficult he was. When I asked her what had happened the night before with Eric, she said she didn't know, that she had just found him in his room, unconscious. Her attitude said that he was just difficult teenager and she had no responsibility in this mess. I tried to say as little as I could. Every step in this conversation was raising my anger level and my desire to lash out. I truly did not want a confrontation with her in his ICU room. Everything was pretty quiet until about midnight when Eric started stirring around. I was ready to light the fireworks. He opened his eyes and looked around and didn't seem to see or recognize me. His eyes locked on his mother. His face got red and started pulling at his restraints.

"You fucking bitch, why didn't you let me die? You can't leave anything alone," he shouted, straining at the restraints. He was trying with all his might to get out of bed. She seemed terrified and said nothing. "You and that asshole Bernie don't care about anything but yourselves. You would both be happier without me."

Chapter 9 – Surrender

I walked around to the far side of his bed and started talking to him softly, stroking the back of this oddly bare head and calmly asked him to lie back down. After a few minutes of this, he lay down but never did acknowledge me. His mother was pressed into the corner of the room and seemed to be in shock.

"See," she said, "I told you he was crazy."

"If you say one more nasty thing about Eric, I'm going to cut his restraints off if he wakes up again," I said. "Why don't you make yourself useful and see if you can find a doctor. They should know about what just happened."

She left the room without saying a word. In spite of the outburst, my spirits soared because in my heart I believed he would make it. And when the doctor came back to the room, he confirmed that it was indeed a good sign. In all likelihood, he was out of his coma. Even though it was my turn to leave the hospital and get some sleep, I suggested that she go home and I would sleep there in the room in the chair. She said nothing, grabbed her coat and left.

At six o'clock the next morning, I awoke to a miracle.

"Hey, when did you get here?" Eric asked with giant smile, while reaching out for my hand. I jumped out of my chair and went to hug him.

"Well Bud, I've been here almost 3 days. Wouldn't have missed this performance for the world."

"Can I come live with you? I can't stand them anymore."

"I'm going to do everything within my power to make that happen."

"Really, I don't think I can go back to that house. I told her over the weekend that I was thinking about killing myself. Monday she took me to see the psychiatrist and they both laughed at me when I said I was planning to kill myself. On Tuesday, I gave it my best try."

"I wasn't just saying that. You will come to Miami and live with me."

In actuality, his next residence was a nearby adolescent psychiatric facility. He was extremely pissed off at me when he found out where he was going. After he tried to disassemble the place his first night, his stay really helped him. When he got out of seclusion, his roommate was a boy of 10 or 12 who had not had a visit from his parents in nearly 6 weeks. This opened Eric's eyes and his heart. The next night was Halloween and there was a party in the unit. He made sure that we got candy and a gift for his roommate. Eric was eventually released back to the world, having been touched most not by his therapy, but by a lovable little boy who had been abandoned to the psychiatric hospital.

Eric made it to Miami in time for Thanksgiving. Unfortunately, his mother had driven him down from Pennsylvania. She was moderately cranky. For her, that passed as a good mood. The first night we went out to dinner to a local Italian restaurant. The dinner was quiet and peaceful until Eric lit up a cigarette and his mother glared at me and asked if I was going to tolerate his behavior. I assured her I was going to tolerate it. She glared. She shouted. We were all asked to leave. Eric and I laughed about that night for a long time.

A new reality was taking shape for me. I finally understood that I had no power or control over the most important things in my life. The notions that I had labored with for 28 years of recovery were exposed in all their weakness. I knew I had wanted power more than faith. My relationship with life and all its pieces was out of order. Somewhere down deep inside of me, I sensed that knowing this was a good thing. I didn't think that this tragedy or near tragedy, was sent to teach Eric or me

Chapter 9 – Surrender

anything. I don't believe God was involved at all. It was a series of awful mistakes ending up in a near tragedy. Of course I can still learn from this! I must have discipline to pursue any difficult path. Must have the courage to commit to action and not hide in the trap of only thinking. I must take action if I'm going to manifest my commitments. My beliefs are found within my actions. I can't say that I believe in the spiritual God while spending 98% of my time pursuing money, property and prestige. Do I have the courage to use only what I need in this life? Can I live a simple life? Can I love people and use things or do I really need to love things and use people?

I had started that night on Coral Way weeks before thinking that evening held some promise. I was comfortable with the thought that my life was in a pretty good place, maybe even a little bit proud. I had people depending on me who had confidence in my ability to make things happen. I had finally found some security in this tumultuous world. The lightning bolt that nearly took my youngest son finally brought me to my knees. I had to surrender to the fact that I had no power in this life to control anything. I was totally dependent on the grace given by my higher power. My arrogant ego was merely an illusion I had manufactured. I've learned that the true nature of the ego is destructive. My path would be to embrace the grace of God and keep love as my focus. Every day I live I am conscious of the gratitude in my heart for the gift of my children. They are the embodiment of God's love in my life.

Chapter 10

Now

And now, my children are okay. I've made my peace with my ex-wife. I am still clean and sober. Through the end of the last chapter I had been sober over 28 years. I was functioning pretty well, I thought. I was however, still not happy. I still thought I needed more. Up to this point, I thought the 'more' I needed was just material things. If I could find just the right combination of things, I would relax and be content. My ego was bloated from its relentless need for reinforcement and affirmation. I believe that I was managing my life as effectively as was humanly possible. I even thought I had a spiritual life. Well, I had a good one to talk about. Wasn't that the point? I guess not. My life was an elegant shambles dressed up by all the convincing talk I had learned in recovery. Fundamental change was needed. Change I had resisted for over 20 years.

What has changed? When I nearly lost my son Eric, every fiber of my life changed. I had been living in a dream world. I had believed a relatively small thing like quitting drinking and drugging created a broad immunity from the perils of life. Although I had been well prepared to stay away from drinking and drugging, I was still clueless regarding living everyday life. For the first time in 28 years, the powerlessness I felt was not a discussion topic but a reality to the depths of my spirit. I experienced it with every one of my senses. I had finally come face-to-face with the great limitations that being human provides. It was clear that I had to take steps to live my life in a new way or I would not be able to live it at all.

Chapter 10 – Now

My belief system told me that if I were to be considered a success in this life, I would have to succeed materially. And while I embraced the notion of a spiritual life in recovery, I was convinced that the sole purpose of the spiritual life was to facilitate material success. This particular belief, and my attachment to it, stopped me from being able to develop any kind of meaningful spiritual life. My higher power had no more presence in my life than a weekly TV show. I was mystified that joy had eluded my life. I was so deserving! A growing part of me was wickedly tired of this pursuit that was so draining and unfulfilling.

Every place I seemed to look for answers (new philosophies, new religions, new relationships, and new jobs) aggravated my stubborn resistance to change. Every way I moved, resulted in my feeling even more bound to the known. AA was still there, a good job was still there, my friends were still there, and change meant I could lose my standing with all of them. Too big of a risk. Inevitably, the flow of life would take over. I lost my job, friends drifted away and AA no longer give me the buzz I sought. I didn't want to drink again. I did, however, think about drugging. It is very strange to be in a body where one side of your personality opines, "You never really had a drug problem, anyway." And the other side pipes up, "Yeah, dummy, two weeks withdrawing from opiates isn't a drug problem, is it?" If somebody else put this bullshit on my plate, I would be furious.

It took two years of intense soul-searching and belief scrubbing to finally open a path that would lead to my spiritual freedom. Everything I had done was clearly not enough. AA was not enough, my approach to higher power was not enough, my work was not enough. I was trying to get gold out of a silver mine. Nothing is wrong with silver. Unless you pretend it is really gold. That would put you on the express train to crazy. My soul kept telling me that what I lacked most was the peace and joy of the spiritual life. Then it pissed me off by telling me I also had to keep working, stay sober and help others. At this point in my life, I was so gut-tired, I just surrendered.

I have meditated for years, primarily as a way to control physical pain, without drugs. The lights came on for me after a short, 10-minute morning meditation. I had been struggling with my need for spiritual change. I didn't know what exactly to change. I knew I wanted to surrender to a higher power. I knew that up to this point I had only made feeble, verbal attempts. Mostly it was window dressing. That morning, I knew that I had simply never trusted my higher power. I had gotten myself too tangled up with religion and its myriad promoters. I knew instantly that I had to stop wading in these spiritual puddles at and dive into the depths. I have a God now. This is my God, he has no followers other than me and you can't have him. Go get your own!

That was easy to write. I should tell you what I actually had to do. It worked for me. I had to reject many things that I had considered life's boilerplate. I had to reject how I had used them. I had to recognize that what went on in my head was not my life. It was just my thoughts about my life. Those thoughts did have the power to make me unhappy. The power of my happiness, and ultimately my joy, came from my actions. My beliefs are mere speculations if I don't turn them into an active part of my daily life. I discovered that talk, although seemingly an active part of life, was much closer to just being loud thoughts. Quoting the "faith without works" parable is not a work of faith. It is a bunch of words most often used to chastise. I find I learn new stuff more readily when I see an example of a concept in practice. Talking about gratitude, isn't gratitude. Treating everyone as a child of God and manifesting joy in that, is gratitude!

When I got sober I thought I didn't have a God. But I had always had a higher power. The power was the belief system that told me what I needed was money property and prestige. That belief system was highly influenced by fear. Any joy generated from these beliefs was fleeting. I believed that everything I needed was outside me. The right job, the right house, the right woman, the right body, and ultimately recognition that I was all right but allow me to relax and enjoy my life. It never

Chapter 10 – Now

occurred to me that this constant, materialistic searching could block the path to spiritual awakening.

Finally, I did as I was told in AA, and created my own God. I created a God that I believe was there before I had an understanding of this God. I believe this God created me out of love, and possessed the power of love. I believe this God had given me everything I needed to function in this world. And a mind so dangerous, I must return it to him. No reservations. No conditions. I believe my job on this planet is to love and be loving. Infuriatingly simple. When I looked at religions, I was overcome by how complicated they were and appalled by their dependence on fear and their addiction to money. I found that a single discipline, philosophy or religion that relied solely on love. So, I chose to go out on my own and just believe in love. And I put every fiber of my being into this love. I am responsible to bring it to every situation I am in. I work on it every day. Most days I fall short. But I still believe it is the right path for me.

Even after 42 years plus of clean and sober living, I still have struggles. At least I know I do now. The character defects I own are not somebody else's that have wandered into my backyard. My character defects do seem to hibernate, only to return in their cranky, hungry and demanding ways. I finally know that they are exclusively my responsibility.

For example, I think I am an extremely forgiving person. The fact is I have not been able to forgive my stepmother and don't know if I ever will. I hate the feeling of being judged by others. And, as soon as they start, I begin judging them. I am close on this one, though. I have accepted that judging others is merely my ego's need to call attention to its own superiority. My ego never has enough.

At one time, the easiest way to capsize my ship of person, was any kind of rejection. Treat me in a way that resembled dismissal and you would ignite my seething rage. Ignore me, or suggest that I was not worthy, and any social grace that I may have had would immediately evaporate. This deadly set of defects would not come under control until I realized I was more the perpetrator then the victim. I realized this while disciplining an employee. I saw hurt and pain in his eyes and realized I was using my position to squash him personally for a rather trivial infraction. I wondered how many times I had done this in the past without ever noticing or caring. I finally appreciate the feelings of others, no matter what the situation.

My life today is run quite differently. While my beliefs have changed radically, my behavior has changed more profoundly. The first area I explored was the not-so-latent negativity behind most of my beliefs. I believed that life was difficult and it was essentially a dangerous place. That little bit of non-wisdom set the stage for my behavior for many years. I found or created evidence to validate this point of view at every turn. I was told I had created this belief and I can almost as easily create a new one. I have set out to do that with fair success. I now believe life is a good opportunity to find and give love and service. It took a couple of years to get over the urge to return to cynicism. Being aware of my ego's desire to overturn my commitment to a positive life, helped a great deal.

I had become aware that AA was not enough. No, I haven't stopped going to meetings or participating in 12 step programs. But at one point, maybe a dozen years ago, I would've told you that living the 12 step life was everything. I can see now, that what it had primarily done, was open all the doors I closed with drinking and drugging and encouraged me to go through them and have a life. There was certain knowledge that I had something to do here and that I needed to be about that business. I don't mean to say that there was anything grand in the cards for me, but I do believe there are vast opportunities that open up once a person stops being a drunken drag on society.

I had to come to terms with, and accept the fact, that for me, less is always better than more. Less food, less space, less demanding and less intrusive behavior. When I started trying to live differently, I had 50

Chapter 10 – Now

shirts in my closet but only wore about six or eight of them. I had a big home that was a source of constant work and worry. I could always identify new wants and needs. I was stuck in the devastating belief that there was something outside me that would make my insides okay. I was way too concerned with what everybody thought. I thought good thoughts and still couldn't fly. My insides would change just as soon as I changed the conduct of my life.

The place that I grew up, Hicksville, New York, was a very blue-collar community. All I thought about was getting out and bettering myself. I now realize that the sense of community in the neighborhood that I lived in, gave me the gold standards for behavior, rather than life. There was rarely a new car to admire and many boats had oars. The force that lived there though was as close as I've ever seen to unconditional love. And it was never talked about. It was just done. Neighbors always looked after neighbors and people smiled at each other. When someone struggled with mental illness, they were not shunned. There were talked to, smiled at and loved.

In my family, love was the only currency. Again, it wasn't a subject for roundtable academic discussion. It was just a fact. With eight children, my parents worked long hours every day of their lives. And yes, they were cranky and tired, at times. But never, ever mean. We had a confidence that was born of knowing we were loved. We lived in a tiny, unadorned tract house but arguments and fights were extremely rare. We laughed with each other, we sang with each other and entertained ourselves with simple things. Our sense of family and its love was all-powerful. It is not possible to replace these feelings with material things. I have no acceptable explanation why I even tried.

I found myself empty after 20 years of sobriety and I dove into meditation. That's a lie. I tiptoed in. (See, I still care about what people think.) I was just blindly running from my life and found what I needed, anyway. Ten minutes in the morning in seated meditation grew after a few months into twenty minutes and has pretty much stayed there for the last twenty-five years.

Sometimes, I will meditate in the early evening when I have the luxury of an extra half hour. At first, all I wanted was for the noise and chaos in my head to stop. It took several months before I realized my practice of meditation was bringing some peace to the war in my head. There was some time and quiet in between my thoughts. I was adjusting to being an observer of my thoughts. I stopped wrestling with them. I let them be.

I got serious about meditation with the expectation that my higher power would talk to me. What would you expect? I was still sick when I started. After the first few months of meditation, I did feel an inner calmness and peace but nothing at all dramatic. I started walking out the door in the morning as a calm, smiling human being. Sometimes it lasted all the way to work. Usually it didn't. This all changed as my rheumatoid arthritis worsened and I became troubled with pain every day. My doctors were more than happy to offer me all the pain meds I wanted. I had absolute clarity that there was no way I could take them safely. One day, in a waiting room at the VA hospital, another patient asked me what I was taking for the pain. I was surprised that he noticed that I was in pain. I told him, "Nothing, I am allergic to opiates and anti-inflammatories don't do much."

He told me he was having good luck calming his pain with meditation. My interest was immediate, but cool. I told him I had been meditating for quite a while and so far, it hadn't seemed to affect my pain. The techniques that he used, he described as being similar to diving deeply into the ocean. He said I would have to completely let go of my need for oxygen and fears. I needed just to go deeper. He said I could use the moment in between thoughts as a diving board into the ocean of my spiritual universe. I went home and tried this for some time with little effect. And then one evening, it was all there.

Chapter 10 – Now

It was in the evening, about seven o'clock. I was physically tired and thought a brief meditation would perk me up for the evening. Just a very few seconds into my meditation, I had a long opening after a thought and I dove in. I was immediately aware of the flow of joy moving over my skin like a light, electrical current. I was in the meditation, I was part of it, not just an observer. The water washed over my skin and I easily aimed downward into the darker blue. It was utterly peaceful. I was aware of absolutely nothing other than that instant. As I traveled deeper into the water, I was startled to see a light glowing in the distance. I had the sensation that I was about to leave everything behind and with that, a germ of fear crept in. I was thinking again. That meditation ended with a sob rising from the depths within me. I had found what I had been looking for. That night, the thought came that I would literally die if I kept swimming toward the brightness in the water. But, I now know that is some kind of boundary that I can open up, freeing me from the incessant dragging of my thoughts. It connects me with a different set of feelings, filling me with the experience of a higher power that has no intellectual vocabulary. Now, I meditate every day. With passion! I may not get to the depths of that first night very often but I'm no longer afraid of the diving board. And my pain is much more manageable!

Service is now the underlying concept that motivates my everyday life. It is the primary vehicle for the delivery of love. It was not always that way. The worm started to turn when I was invited to go to prison. By my sponsor, not the state. The first time I went, was to put on a party for inmates at a maximum-security prison in Michigan. It was Christmas Eve and I was extremely put out to have to spend my time with criminals, instead of my family. There were four other men in the car for the 100-mile drive across Michigan in a light snow. They actually appeared to be jolly and happy to be spending Christmas Eve in a prison. I sat in my self-pity and chain smoked for the entire two-hour ride. I even had the nerve to be offended when none of them tried to cheer me up.

We arrived at the prison almost 2 hours before the meeting was scheduled to start. I, of course, managed to complain about this to everyone. I tried to warm up a little by asking my sponsor what most of the guys at the meeting were imprisoned for. And he said, "Mostly killing."

I just looked at him and said nothing. And he said, "Most of them don't even remember doing it, they were drunk." Then, we got to sign the presence disclaimer. Basically, it said that if there was a riot or any sort of problem, they couldn't guarantee our safety. I seriously thought about waiting in the car but couldn't imagine asking my sponsor for the keys.

We had a typical meeting for Christmas Eve. We sat in a circle and shared our gratitude for sobriety and the life we now had. I was thinking how difficult it was for me to be grateful as I listened to these men open their hearts and share real gratitude, although few of them would ever see freedom again. As they opened up, I was more and more surprised at how little difference there was between them and me. No, I hadn't killed anybody but I could have very easily. I was an angry and violent drunk. It could easily be me that wouldn't get to go home that night. We served cake and ice cream and socialized almost an hour. I was surprised to find my main emotion on the way home was sadness.

The prison was the beginning of my acceptance that I wasn't better than anybody. If I was to have a spiritual life, I had to embrace the opportunity to serve everyone no matter what his or her situation might be. I now start my day with prayers to help me identify opportunities… to identify the people and the moments that have been set in my path for me to provide service…for me to understand that the only attitude of value I can bring to life, is giving. The understanding has finally reached me, that through the gift of loving others, I make myself worthy of their love…and the joy that lives only in that world of love.

Chapter 10 – Now

My existence now at its simple level appears to be what I am designed for. My higher power tugged at me for years to get my attention. I now accept that peace exists only at the simplest levels of human activity and love can only flow from that peace. I am happy and am made whole through my fellow man, in my gratitude for being allowed to serve them. I am allowed and encouraged to love. My day begins and ends with prayer and meditation, energizing my life for the grateful service opportunity that each day holds. May you each find your God and take his hand for your life!